truth about ROCK

STEVE PETERS ⊹
MARK LITTLETON

truth about ROCK

BETHANY HOUSE PUBLISHERS
MINNEAPOLIS, MINNESOTA 55438

The Truth About Rock
Copyright © 1998
Steve Peters & Mark Littleton

Cover design by The Lookout Design Group

Published by Bethany House Publishers
A Ministry of Bethany Fellowship International
11300 Hampshire Avenue South
Minneapolis, Minnesota 55438

Printed in the United States of America by
Bethany Press International, Minneapolis, Minnesota 55438

Library of Congress Cataloging-in-Publication Data

Peters, Steve.
    The truth about rock : shattering the myth of harmless music / by Steve
Peters & Mark Littleton.
        p.   cm.
    ISBN 0–7642–2053–5 (pbk.)
    1. Rock music—History and criticism. 2. Rock music—Reviews. 3. Music
and morals. 4. Rock music—Religious aspects—Christianity. I. Littleton,
Mark R., 1950–   . II. Title.
ML3534.P475   1997
781.66—dc21
                                                                97–33957
                                                                       CIP
                                                                       MN

I wish to thank my lovely wife,

Julie,

for standing with me for sixteen years, for believing in me and helping to make me what I am today. Thanks, Julie, for helping us reach over three million kids with the Truth About Rock seminars. God won't forget the many years we spent on the road sharing this vital message. I can't forget my children,

Stefanie and Benjamin,

who have blessed me again and again.

—Steve

———

To

Nicole and Alisha,

my daughters, who often open my eyes
to the truth by their
winsome, loving ways.

—Mark

Publisher's Note

Some of the quoted lyrics and documentation in this book are sexually explicit and offensive. Though the authors and publisher would prefer not to include these quotations, it seems to be the only way to convey to the public the severity and reality of some of today's rock music content. We recommend parents and youth leaders observe caution in the use of this material.

We believe this book to be a very important "red alert" for the society in which we live. We hope it will serve to expose the truth about today's rock music culture.

If you have any observations or questions about the contents of this work, we invite you to write to the authors or to Bethany House Publishers.

Acknowledgments

This book is another milestone in my life. So much has happened since my brother Dan and I wrote *Why Knock Rock?* and *What About Christian Rock?* in the mid-1980s. So many people have blessed my life and help bring the best out in me.

To my mom and dad, who set an unwavering Christian example for me through the years . . . I love you! To my brother Jim, my coworker in Christ who helped launch this ministry in 1979 and now directs GTM Ministries—thanks for caring. To my brother Dan, the visionary, who helped us touch the world, it's been a great ride. Guys, we'll see many in heaven because we worked together.

I want to acknowledge the love, support, and friendship we have received from our church, Destiny Christian Center in Burnsville, Minnesota. Pastor Joe Braucht has been a great friend. My Promise Keepers Bible study group has kept me accountable. Thanks to Pastor Hank Davis for his wisdom. I'm grateful to Lisa Kroehler, Jean Gardner, Paula Johnson, and many others who did a ton of research and computer entry.

We've had a long run with Bethany House Publishers, who believed in us when other publishers didn't and in so doing helped launch our nationwide ministry. We still get many letters with comments from readers of *Why Knock Rock?*, our first book published years ago, and pastors requesting one of our seminars. Thank you!

Special thanks to my coauthor, Mark Littleton, who can take what I want to say, combine it with reams of research, organize it, and commit it to paper. And to Kevin Johnson, our editor at Bethany

House, for his years of expertise that have sharpened this book—thanks. I'm grateful to Steve Laube and Christopher Soderstrom for their editorial input, expertise, and many hours invested into this project.

And God bless the kids in my youth group from 1972–1982 at Zion Christian Center, who forced me to learn the youth culture and discover secular music. Those lessons culminated in this ministry.

So many people have blessed my life that the pages in this book couldn't contain all the names. Thank you for touching my life in so many ways.

Finally, to the readers—including skeptics, believers, agnostics, and atheists—I trust you too will discover the truth about rock!

Steve J. Peters

Contents

CHAPTER ONE

A Short History of a Big Subject

"Wild Bill" Moore gave us the words in a rinky-tink, rattlin' guitar-backed song that said, "We're gonna rock; we're gonna roll." It was a bit of spice then, but it wasn't until 1952 that Alan Freed, a deejay in Cleveland, coined the words and made them famous. He had been playing some new sounds on his late afternoon program, *Moondog Matinee*. He dubbed the style "rock 'n' roll."

Suddenly a whole new musical genre was born. Freed went on to New York City to play his tunes on WABC, one of the largest radio stations in the U.S. at the time. From 1956 to 1959 he appeared in rock movies, introduced the latest tunes on his TV program, *The Big Beat*, and even coauthored a number of hits.

But it was not to last—at least not for Freed. In 1959 a payola scandal struck Freed at the core. He had been promoting new singers and groups while taking kickbacks. In the middle of a song by Little Anthony and the Imperials, "Shimmy Shimmy Ko-Ko-Bop," Freed cut in, sobbing out the news that he'd just resigned as a result of the scandal. Five years later he died at the age of forty-two, drunk and broke, in a Florida hospital. The man who named an era was its first victim.

But rock wasn't to be halted by a scandal or two. Names like Bill

Haley, Chuck Berry, and Buddy Holly climbed the charts. Everywhere, it seemed, people were "rockin' around the clock." Everywhere, screaming fans met their heroes on tour, sang their songs, and bought their records. Rock 'n' roll had become big business.

Along with the "good times" and the I'm-just-joking angle of much of what was written and sung, other themes crept into rock's growing repertoire, especially that of sexual innuendo. Chuck Berry's "Maybellene" was filled with suggestive lyrics not lost on teen fans. Little Richard's "Good Golly, Miss Molly" raised the roof and topped the charts, but at its heart was praise for Molly's sexual appetite: "Good golly, Miss Molly, sure like to ball." Little Richard dodged the charge that he was suggesting sex by saying it was all about dancing. But in street slang "ball" meant sexual intercourse. This sleight of hand was not lost on fans, either.

At the same time, Jerry Lee Lewis began wowing fans with stage antics such as throwing chairs and playing the piano with his feet. His songs "Whole Lotta Shakin' Goin' On" and "Great Balls of Fire" were filled with a sexual tango that made him not only a star but a sex object. Nonetheless, rock 'n' roll was still not immune to scandal. When Lewis's marriage to his thirteen-year-old cousin became known, the media and the public wrote him off and his popularity plummeted. Rock personalities didn't even like to smoke in front of fans for fear the behavior would impinge on their image.

Buddy Holly was next to hit the big time and big bucks, and he managed to produce clean-lyricked tunes such as "Maybe Baby," "Peggy Sue," and "Reminiscing." However, each of them had suggestive overtones, which were muted enough for airplay but not misunderstood by fawning fans. His death in a plane crash with Richie Valens, another up-and-comer, was called years later by Don McLean "the day the music died" in his rock anthem "American Pie."

Strangely, many of these performers suffered serious setbacks that put their careers on the backset. Chuck Berry spent time in jail, Little Richard got religious and went to seminary, Buddy Holly died in a plane crash, and Jerry Lee Lewis hit a definite downbeat in his career. Rock fans were searching for a new symbol on the horizon, and Elvis Presley was about to fill the bill.

Presley was (and to many still is) the "King of Rock 'n' Roll." After his first hit, "Heartbreak Hotel," in 1956, he was established as the heir to the adulation of fans, nationally and internationally. Arnold Shaw in his *Dictionary of American Pop/Rock* shows the impact Presley had in a multitude of ways:

> Presley represented not only a new sound but a new look (sideburns and ducktail haircut), new dress (blue suede shoes), new sensibility (the sneer), new mores (a more sensual approach to love), new speech ("all shook up"), and new dances. His hysterical acceptance was the expression of a young generation in conflict with and in rebellion against the older generation.[1]

Elvis "the pelvis" scored six gold records the first year after "Heartbreak Hotel." Presley's animal-like sexuality drew out of his audiences not only adulation but a spontaneous, salacious response. Every girl on the street wanted Elvis for a boyfriend and lover.

At the same time, the older generation woke up. This snortin', snarlin' stallion of a singer was changing the way young people looked at life. Suddenly the triumvirate of school, family, and church had lost meaning. All that mattered was looking, acting, listening to, and being like Elvis. Pastors, parents, and newspaper editors took notice and began preaching against the rebelliousness that Presley symbolized. Something had to be done.

Something was done. Colonel Parker, Elvis's crafty, culture-savvy manager, advised Elvis to report for a preinduction physical for the army. This public relations coup won points both with fans and with parents.

But then the unthinkable happened: Elvis was drafted. That was never Colonel Parker's plan, but Elvis spent two years in Germany after boot camp. When he returned, he shed his hip-swiveling image for that of a Las Vegas showman. His kingship became secure as the greatest live entertainer on earth, and his fans adored him.

In the '60s Elvis was forced aside by the advent of another band of culture-setters: the Beatles. With his career in eclipse, Elvis turned to syrupy ballads ("In the Ghetto") while becoming addicted to drugs. He died in August 1977 with fourteen different drugs pulsing through his body. Since his death, however, Presley has actually become more famous. His estate, valued at less than 10 million dollars when he died, was parlayed into a multimillion-dollar industry by his ex-wife, Priscilla Presley, and her advisors. Today the Elvis music and peripherals empire, including Graceland, a virtual shrine for many Elvis-worshipers, is worth nearly a billion dollars.

But bigger things were on the horizon. Rock 'n' roll didn't end with Elvis. In fact, he laid the groundwork for the British invasion, the Beatles, and the coming of some of the most lauded rock musicians in history.

Between Elvis in the late '50s and the Beatles in the early '60s, a long list of one-hit wonders and overnight sensations struck with names like Richie, Tab, Fabian, Joey, and Bobby. Teens bought the records and the industry grew. But behind the scenes, the real action took place. Hustlers and hucksters made their mark, often buying off lifetime rights to songs from their composers. Dick Clark of *American Bandstand* and numerous others profiteered from the rock racket, while rock musicians scuttled up the silver-lined clouds of notoriety one day and down the black hole of obscurity the next. Producers and record companies sucked in the bucks while the musicians made it with the girls. Organized crime made millions wooing deejays with drugs, loose women, and payola. Everyone seemed happy on top, but the underside of the rock world was as black as sin. Songwriter Linton Kwesi Johnson put it this way:

> The music business is one of the nastiest, dirtiest businesses in the world. It seems to be very fertile ground for con men and tricksters, all kinds of ruthless and unscrupulous people. I suppose because there's so much money to be picked up. It's a dirty, stinking business.[2]

When the Beatles hit the scene in the '60s, the tunes were innocuous enough: "Love Me Do," "She Loves You," and "I Want to Hold Your Hand." It was just love and fun. They had a lock on the charts. Nearly everything they produced went gold. Paul McCartney and John Lennon weren't plugged into the culture as much as the culture was plugged into them. In a few short years, they produced more singalong songs than any singer or songwriter has since. Young people could wile away an evening washing dishes in a restaurant while singing the Beatles' hits. The songs were memorable and gripping.

But there was a stench rising in the kingdom. As early as 1964, the Fab Four were using marijuana. By 1967, with the release of "Sgt. Pepper's Lonely Hearts Club Band," the Beatles' commitment to drugs was well known. John Lennon claimed to have tripped on LSD a thousand times. When he needed to record new music, he took speed.

This attitude had an astonishing effect on the American public. Suddenly marijuana, speed, and LSD were "cool," "in," "the thing to do." Songs like "Lucy in the Sky With Diamonds," allegedly for the acronym LSD, were only pleasurable if you were zonked while you listened to them. College campuses were affected first. Then the college kids came home and "turned on" their high school friends. Drugs filtered through everything. Kids came home stoned out of their heads, then sat down with Mom and Dad and watched *Laugh-In*. Parents didn't know anything was up. They merely thought their son or daughter really enjoyed the program.

The press kept out of it. They concealed the truth about the Beatles' lifestyle because they not only liked the mop-tops but the Beatles knew how to keep them in tow. They invited the media people to their parties where the reefers were piled on tea tables next to the smaller piles of poison—LSD, amphetamines, mescaline, heroin, cocaine, and other signature drugs that went by names like "California Gold," "Kentucky Jasmine," and "JuJuBee." In effect, the Beatles became drug "evangelists," spreading the "gospel" of peace, love, and nonviolence. At the same time, John Lennon was beating his wife.

After the drugs, as the cynicism and bitterness of life without meaning caught up with them, the Beatles took a religious turn. They found their guru in Maharishi Mahesh Yogi, a Hindu philosopher with a new idea: Transcendental Meditation. So caught up were the Beatles in Maharishi's philosophy that George Harrison wrote the hit song "My Sweet Lord" to praise his master. Eventually, though, Lennon and the others soured on Maharishi as a fake. Only

Harrison held on and continued to practice TM and plug its ideas into his music.

As other bands caught on from Britain and America, the antics on stage grew more decadent. Jim Morrison of the Doors exposed himself. Mick Jagger of the Rolling Stones pranced and strutted like a rooster telling his hens to line up.

The Vietnam War heated things up, and a radical resistance to it was fostered by rock stars such as Country Joe and the Fish, the Grateful Dead, and Jefferson Airplane. This era of protest, drugs, and "free love" was epitomized during the Woodstock Festival in 1969. The music kept playing, but for what? Many of the top bands had opted for nihilism: "If it feels right, do it" and "Whatever turns you on."

Mama Cass of The Mamas and the Papas said, "Pop music is just long hours, hard work, and lots of drugs. . . ."[3]

The '70s saw movement from pop sounds to heavy metal, and bands like Led Zeppelin, Black Sabbath, Grand Funk Railroad, and MC5 made their mark as the loudest and the raunchiest. Black Sabbath introduced themselves to the press with a "party" featuring the mock sacrifice of a semi-nude girl. They touted the Devil and talked endlessly about what it was like serving him. The Eagles wrote "Hotel California," which many believe was an ode to the Devil and a witches' coven in Los Angeles.

As the '70s moved into a phase of who could be the toughest and the nastiest, other groups came on the scene like KISS. Dressed in makeup and outfits bizarre enough to match their devil-lauding lyrics, they subjected their fans to mind-grinding beats and megadecibel guitar riffs. If you didn't get high on the fumes of the drugs being smoked around you, you got dazed by the pulsation of the music. It filled your bones and made you want to dance.

The late '70s saw the advent of punk rock with the Sex Pistols and other groups bent on getting "down and ugly" with their audiences. Often their concerts degenerated into spitting and vomiting contests between the performers and the audience. Violence on the stage and in the box seats became the norm, and frequently people were trampled or maimed in the ruckus that inevitably occurred.

Iggy Pop slashed himself in the chest. The Sex Pistols screamed obscenities and sparred with fans. Their music extolled homosexuality, bestiality, lesbianism, sodomy, masochism, transvestitism, and a smattering of other topics that at one time had seemed *verboten*. But the cat and the lyrics were definitely out of the bag.

The late '70s also saw disco become the rage. In the '80s rock began to broaden to take on new styles such as shock rock and new wave. It was an ever-changing medium, constantly reinventing itself. Madonna sang her naughty songs, such as "Like a Virgin" and "Vogue," and wore brass-spiked bras at her concerts, flaunting her sexuality and taunting the crowd with a smooth come-on.

Michael Jackson, a far cry from his adolescent days with The Jackson Five, performed androgynously, did the moonwalk, and sang "Beat it," "Thriller," and "Bad," twisting his lyrics into anthems for teenage rebellion.

John Hinckley Jr., a punk rock aficionado, had attended a Kamikaze Klones concert the night before he attempted to assassinate President Reagan. There he listened to songs like "Death Can Be Fun" and "Psycho Killer." Rock 'n' roll had taken a weird and malicious turn for the worse.

Out of the morass grew such styles as death-funk, psycho pop, grunge, and themes too numerous to count. As rock moved into the late '80s with bands like Nirvana chugging out their suicidal lyrics, nobody seemed to care or notice. There were still Whitney Houston, Michael Bolton, Don Henley, Bruce Springsteen, and many others to fill the gap. It seemed that rock reinvented itself over and over like a chameleon gone wild.

Yet there was no stopping it. Today rock is a 40 billion-dollar industry with everything from CDs and tapes to videos, sweat shirts, underwear, stickers, posters, and everything else you can imagine. You hear it played in the malls, drugstores, dentist offices, and blasting from the car next to you at a stoplight.

Consider these facts:

- There are 14.8 million teenagers in America today.
- Teenagers buy more music each year than any other age group.

- Rock/Alternative music made up more than one-third of all music sold in the U.S. last year.
- Drug use among those twelve to seventeen years of age has risen almost eighty percent since 1992.
- The suicide rate among teens has risen 120% in the last fifteen years.
- Thirty-four percent of teens have sex because movies or TV make it seem normal.[4]

We must ask these questions about rock music: Is it good? Is it bad? Is it neutral? What is a Christian to say and do about its ever-changing, ever-growing, and ever-grasping influence? How can we be around it but not *of* it, as the apostle Paul tells us we are to be in the world but not of it?

That is precisely what the rest of this book is about.

Notes

1. Arnold Shaw, *Dictionary of American Pop/Rock* (New York: Macmillan, 1982), 287.
2. Gary Herman, *Rock 'n' Roll Babylon* (Great Britain: Plexus Publishing Ltd., 1982), 25.
3. Ibid., 63.
4. Taken from *The Recording Industry Association of America; Time Magazine; Newsweek;* and *Al Menconi's Media Update* as quoted in a retail sales training booklet from Sublime Records, February 1998, page 3.

CHAPTER TWO

Lyrics: It's All in a Song

The October 13, 1997, issue of *Time* magazine carried the tragic story of a sexually abused fifteen-year-old named Sam Manzie. He raped and murdered eleven-year-old Eddie Werner. What exactly happened?

Werner was selling decorative wrapping paper and candy for his middle school in hopes of winning a set of walkie-talkies. When he happened to knock on Manzie's door, the fifteen-year-old invited him in, then raped and strangled him and hid his body in a suitcase to dispose of later. Manzie himself was sexually abused by a pedophile named Stephen Simmons, age forty-three, of Holbrook, New York. Manzie had met Simmons in a chat room on the Internet.

The immediate blame for the murder belongs to Manzie, a troubled youth whose parents tried unsuccessfully only days before to have him committed to a psychiatric unit. The judge refused, calling the boy "a fine young man."

But *Time* cited several other sources of larger blame. The writers of the article asked several pointed questions:

> Community members and the local press were quick to ascribe larger blame for the horrid crime. Shouldn't the unregulated Internet be made accountable? Or the *depressing lyrics of the rock songs* Sam Manzie loved? (italics mine).

Manzie, a bright boy, created his own web page on which he

"told of his passion for the band Smashing Pumpkins."[1] While trying to prove an actual connection between Smashing Pumpkins' "angst-ridden" lyrics[2] and Manzie's actions would be futile, what should be plain is that a boy in need of friendship while listening constantly to depressing music could easily conclude there's nothing good in the world. He might begin to take out the resultant anger and frustration in violent action. And that is precisely what he did.

Proverbs 23:7 tells us, "As a man thinketh in his heart, so is he." The thoughts and ideas we program into our brain have an effect on us. They influence and produce who we truly become as people. If we listen to, meditate upon, and repeat words that are evil, our thoughts will become evil. Thoughts soon lead to words and words to actions.

For this reason, lyrics are *extremely* important. In modern rock music, one can be soothed by mesmerizing lines of peace and goodness or whipped into a frenzy by wild, erotic, or violent words challenging the listener to commit or applaud foul deeds.

Lyrics matter. They stick. Young people can recite whole songs from memory that they listened to years ago, while often they can't tell you one thing they learned in school today, or even the whole year.

Lyrics have an impact. They dance and jangle and glitter in the mind like unfurled flags telling us either that "God is so good" or to "Go to hell. . . ." depending on whom you are listening to. While some lyrics to the eye might look innocuous, imagine them set to the pulsations of a hard-edged guitar, angry voices, a pounding beat, or a heart-caressing melody.

In this chapter, we will offer a quick study of the kinds of lyrics you will find in secular rock music today. What are young people listening to? What ideas and philosophies are they bombarded with as they flick the radio dial to their favorite stations? What "truths" are they planting into their outlook as they mentally drink in the music and the message and video images of the "heroes" on their bedroom walls?

The "Life Stinks" Riff

The belief that life on our planet is meaningless and empty is a common theme in much of today's music. It started with a whisper in Beatles' cuts like "Eleanor Rigby" and "A Day in the Life" and has continued in the dirges and rages of groups like Nirvana and KORN. Despair, sadly enough, is very popular. Young people buy into it, quickly and gladly. Their favorite bands unleash their anger at school, their parents, their girlfriends and boyfriends, the government, and everyone else.

Consider some of these lyrics from popular bands:

Bush. This band "links rage and erotica, portrays life as miserable and meaningless." The song "Bomb" shouts, "Blow me away, see if I care . . . kill a man; kill a girl."[3]

The Cure. Their music's called "miserable, obsessed with death and mope rock." Robert Smith is "a virtual messiah of gloom" and has died seventy-four times in their songs. Even *Rolling Stone* asks, "Is life as bleak as their brooding lyrics suggest?"[4]

The punk rock band The Offspring has an album called "Ixnay on the Hombre." It's full of obscenities, angst, and meaninglessness. In "The Meaning of Life" there's no meaning or truth available, so you do what you want:

> *If all of this seems to say there's no right and wrong way.*
> *Sorry if I don't feel like living the way you do.*

In "Mota" they escape into drugs to find meaning and peace:

> *That bong that's on the table starts to call my name.*
> *I take a hit and zone out again . . .*
> *losing out might feel okay all night.*

In "Cool to Hate" they end up hating everything and everybody:

> *I never have nothing good to say.*
> *I'd rather tear things down than build them up. . . .*
> *I'm only happy when I'm in my misery, so f—— you!*

Nine Inch Nails is the group sometimes called the master of glum rock. It thrives on depression and pain. "They push brutal waves of chaos on foreboding vocals and taboo subject matter."[5]

The group's songs and albums include "Mr. Self-Destruct," "Sin-Dead Souls," "Head Like a Hole," "Happiness in Slavery," and "The Downward Spiral."

The lead singer, Trent Reznor, embraces "sex and death . . . links anger and violence to a sexually charged experience suggesting drag, camp, even homosexuality."[6]

Of course, the masters of disaster, Nirvana, led by Kurt Cobain, now dead by his own hand, pioneered the grunge rock sound of Seattle. Cobain became an instant celebrity, but he was a tormented soul. His music repeatedly plumbs the themes of alienation, emptiness, nihilism, and deep despair. He composed and sang songs like "I Hate Myself and Want to Die." In his final rock tour in Europe, he climbed a bank of speakers and threatened to hurl himself into the crowd, committing suicide.

What happens to a young mind when he listens to and fills his life with such twisted ideas? The apostle Paul warned us in the book of Colossians: "Set your minds on things above, not on earthly things" (3:2). What are the things of earth? John put it this way: "Do not love the world or anything in the world. . . . For everything in the world—the cravings of sinful man, the lust of his eyes and the boasting of what he has and does—comes not from the Father but from the world" (1 John 2:15–16). When the average teen spends at least six hours a day listening to rock, it is bound to have an effect. Something has to give—either their mind or their faith. Usually it's both.

Kill Me, Kill You, Kill Everybody

A second theme in modern rock lyrics is a fascination with violence, suicide, death, hatred, and rage. This goes from story songs of actual acts of violence to the brutal and plainspoken advocacy of going and doing likewise.

KORN produced an album called "Life Is Peachy," which debuted at number three on the charts. However, this rage, anger, and despair band doesn't think life is at all peachy. The lead singer, Jonathan Davis, has three singing styles: "whine, moan, and psychotic scream," according to *Home Life* magazine. In the song "Good God," it is not clear whom it is they hate, but they certainly do not espouse Jesus' command to "love your enemies":

> *How could you take away everything that I was,*
> *to be your f——ing slave.*
> *Your face I despise . . .*
> *Get the f—— out of my life.*

The last song on the album, "Kill You," screeches hate words toward parents with the refrain, "All I want to do is kill you."

The Dead Kennedys sing the following words on one of their albums:

> *I kill children.*
> *I love to see them die.*
> *I kill children*
> *and make their mamas cry.*
> *Crush 'em under my car;*
> *I want to hear them scream.*
> *Feed 'em poison candy*
> *to spoil their Halloween.*
> *I kill children. . . .*
> *I can hardly wait for yours.*[7]

When I debated Jello Biafra, lead singer of the Dead Kennedys, in front of an extremely hostile audience, he claimed I was misinterpreting his lyrics. I responded, "I'm not interpreting, I'm just reading them." Another one of his songs, "Too Drunk to F——," has few lyrics besides the title set to head-banging music.

Metallica, a heavy metal band whose fans have filled whole stadiums, sings in "Harvester of Sorrow":

> *Drink up, shoot up*
> *Let the beating begin,*
> *Distributor of pain.*
> *Your loss becomes my gain;*
> *To see into my eyes*
> *You'll find where murder lies.*
> *Infanticide.*

Bob Larson, a national talk show host, says this band fosters "violence among their head banger listeners. . . . Tunes celebrate suicide, hatred, and hopelessness."[8]

KRS-One, a rap group, speaks of killing a police officer:

> On the ground was a bottle of Snapple
> I broke the bottle in his f——ing Adam's apple.
> His partner called for backup,
> I had the shotgun and began to act up
> With that "bo-bo-bo, kak-kak-kak":
> The only way to deal with racism
> If you're black.

Coolio, another rapper, glorifies "gangsta" violence. In "Recoup This" the artist shoots his agent and secretary over money. He makes violent threats in "Gangsta's Paradise." *Plugged In*, a magazine about popular youth culture,[9] states that Coolio's music exploits urban decay and is both "lewd and irresponsible."[10]

Pearl Jam, according to *Parental Guidance*, sings of "despair, misery, and isolation. . . . Relies on profanity and oral sex for added shock value. . . . [and] speaks of suicide as a viable answer to life's problems."[11]

Even the recently knighted Sir Elton John, of "Lion King" and "Candle in the Wind" fame, does not flinch at singing of such taboo subjects as suicide:

> I'm getting bored
> being part of mankind,
> think I'll buy a forty-four
> and give 'em all a sunrise.
> Yeah, think I'm gonna kill myself,
> cause a little suicide. . . .

Steven Tyler, lead singer of the band Aerosmith, recently rejected his role as an antihero. He said, "I don't want the responsibility of some young kid trying to live his life like I did back in the '70s."[12] Yet amid graphic sexual references, he advocates brutal violence:

> I wake you up with an axe . . .
> I'll leave your bullet-ridden body
> on the curb.

The band Obituary has songs such as "Bloodsoaked," "Suffocation," and "Deadly Intention" that are all paragons of violence and rage. They say, "We believe in the power of metal and our music is a testament to that." Reviewers agree they are demented.[13]

Scarface had a number one, best-selling record in early 1997 called "The Untouchable." He's a foul-mouthed "gangsta rapper," a former member of the Geto Boys. In his songs he totes guns, kills his foes, and strings obscenities together like cheap beads. The hate-charged album contains such lyrics as these:

Sunshine,
I'll blow your brains.
[I'm] your f——in' terror
and you ain't seen me coming.
No death like this ever semi-automatic
exploding between your eyes.

Apparently, Scarface has learned nothing from the deaths of Tupac Shakur and The Notorious B.I.G., both of whose hate-filled partisan albums contributed to their early deaths at the hands of gunmen.

Guns N' Roses made no apology for their own references to killing. In "Used to Love Her," lead singer Axl Rose sang:

I used to love her,
but I had to kill her.
I had to put her six feet under
And I can still hear her complain.
I knew I'd miss her,
so I had to keep her.
She's buried right in my backyard.

After complaints from women that this song promoted the murder of females, the band pled innocence, claiming that the song is about killing their pet dog. Considering that no one buries their dog that deep ("six feet under"), the possibility remains that these lyrics were written merely for shock value. Glorifying a violent act and adding a horror movie spin.

The Prodigy had a hit song off their album "Fat of the Land" called "Smack My B——ch Up." WalMart and K-Mart pulled the

album from their shelves after receiving complaints from the National Organization of Women (NOW). Of course, The Prodigy
claims the single has nothing to do with violence toward women.[14]
Is their song about a dog too?

Many bands move from storytelling to outright challenge, such
as "Suicide's an Alternative" by Suicidal Tendencies:

> *Sick of life—it sucks.*
> *Sick and tired—no one cares.*
> *Sick of myself—don't wanna live.*
> *Sick of living—gonna die.*
> *Suicide's an alternative!*

Consider a boy of fifteen or so listening to such refrains over
and over, six hours a day. If a fifteen-second commercial can have a
mass effect played several times a week or month, consider the impact of this type of music on the brain of someone who listens to it
for hours a day.

To support such rockers by buying their albums, plastering their
pictures on bedroom walls, and talking of them as if they were the
great folk heroes of our time, is a travesty that borders on blasphemy.
The prophet says, "Should you help the wicked and love those who
hate the Lord? Because of this, the wrath of the Lord is upon you"
(2 Chron. 19:2).

Let Me Abuse Myself

If nihilism and violence are large themes in rock, what looms
even larger is drugs and alcohol. Many rockers see nothing wrong
with getting high, whether it's marijuana, cocaine, heroin, or whiskey. And they'll tell you as much in their songs. For instance, Sheryl
Crow sings about Ouija boards and booze, one-night stands, that
abortion is okay, and "I still get stoned."[15]

Green Day, a punk rock band, composes lyrics about pot, boredom, and sex. Their "Dookie" album's first single, "Longview," was
an ode to two time-honored standbys: apathy and masturbation.[16]
They believe in saying yes to drugs—alcohol, speed, and marijuana.

Mike Dirnt, a member of the band, said, "I think doing drugs are very important. I was flying on acid so hard . . ."[17] Tre Cool, another band member, added, "People bring weed to our shows; that's wonderful. . . ." And the third member, Billie Joe Armstrong, had this to chip in: "I have an alcohol problem. . . . Our main choice is speed."

Tom Petty, with his band, the Heartbreakers, sings in "You Don't Know How It Feels," "Let's roll another joint." Amazingly, MTV censored the video. This was on a cable program where you can find a regular fare of sex scenes, near nudity, and even flatulence. Yet, though teens could watch MTV's footage of Woodstock II crowd members tripping on acid and downing beer, rolling another joint was too much for them.[18]

Government statistics show that there's a revival among teens and even younger kids who are beginning to use marijuana, LSD, cocaine, and other drugs. But alcohol remains the drug of choice for most. Why do so many young people find the lure impossible to resist? Could part of the reason be that they hear their rock heroes singing of the glories of the high and want to emulate them?

Robert Coles, Harvard child psychologist and author of *The Moral Life of Children*, writes, "If strong family or church life is absent, what other moral influences are there? Children take what they see in the media to be the adult world in operation—they tell you that!"

David Elkind, Ph.D., another child psychologist and author of *The Hurried Child*, says, "Clearly, the most underestimated influence on young people today is the record business. . . . We prefer to ignore the impact of rock music on our offspring. As a culture, we are visually-oriented and this is why we are so concerned about the sex and violence presented on television and in films. But music can influence young people as much as any visual media."

The Three-Letter Universal Rock Theme: S-E-X

If violence and drugs rue the day in rock's hallowed halls, it's sex that rules. As early as 1967, Andrew Oldham, manager of the Rolling

Stones, said, "Rock music is sex and you have to hit them [teenagers] in the face with it."[19]

Debbie Harry of the now defunct rock band Blondie said in *Circus* magazine, "Rock 'n' roll is all sex. One hundred percent. Sometimes music can make you come."[20]

Here are some examples of sexual lyrics in modern rock:

Tone Loc gets very down and dirty in "Wild Thing," which reached number two on the charts:

> *Could not get her off my jock.*
> *She was like static cling.*
> *That's what happens*
> *When bodies start slappin'*
> *From doing the wild thing.*

Janet Jackson, Michael's younger sister who has made it almost as big in rock today as Michael himself, relies on sexual sighs that "build to an orgasmic, S——!" on "Throb." "If" alludes to oral sex. "Anytime, Anyplace" depicts public sex.

Paula Abdul uses sensual, suggestive, and erotic lyrics in such songs as "Head Over Heels," "Get Your Groove On," and "Sexy Thoughts."

The Spice Girls, a global sensation from Britain, sing on "Wannabe:"

> *If you wannabe my lover,*
> *you've got to get with my friends.*

The tabloids, in searching through the backgrounds of the girls, found that one, Geri, posed for nude pictures in her teens. She commented: "I wanted to get my t—— out and go running naked in the woods."[21]

The Artist, formerly known as Prince, praises incest on his "Purple Rain" album:

> *My sister never made love*
> *to anyone but me.*
> *Incest is everything*
> *it's said to be.*

"Darling Nikki" describes Prince's sexual encounter with a girl he met "in a hotel lobby masturbating with a magazine."

ZZ Top speaks of a lover in "Under Pressure":

She don't like other women . . .
She likes whips and chains . . .
She likes cocaine . . .

"I Want Your Sex," by George Michael, encourages his listeners to give in to their sexual urges:

I said I won't tease you
Won't tell you no lies
Don't need no Bible,
just look in my eyes.
I've waited so long, baby,
out in the cold,
But I can't take much more, girl,
I'm losing control.
I want your sex, I want your love,
I want your sex, I want your sex . . .

2 Live Crew rapper Mark Ross said the lyrics on their "As Nasty As They Wanna Be" album were meant to be funny, not dirty. Songs on the album include "Dick Almighty," "Bad A——— B——ch," and "Me So Horny." A Broward County, Florida judge said the lyrics appeared to be obscene, and the rap group sued in federal court. To make his point to the federal judge, Ross quoted lines of "Me So Horny," lyrics that are tame compared with some their others:

You can say I'm desperate,
Even call me perverted,
But you say I'm a dog
When I leave you f——ed and deserted.

The judge wasn't amused. He ruled the music obscene.[22]

In "Saving All My Love for You," Whitney Houston's lyrics find pleasure in adultery:

A few stolen moments
is all we share.
You've got your family,
and they need you there.

> *Though I try to resist*
> *being last on your list . . .*
> *So I'm saving all my love for you.*
> *We'll be making love*
> *the whole night through.*

Experts say that there's a new element in music—a meanness of spirit and outright hatred—that wasn't present in the early days of rock 'n' roll. Rap music, in particular, seethes with sex that includes violence, hatred, and the debasing of women. The following are some examples:

"We Want Some P——sy"
2 Live Crew

> *Hey, we want some p——sy.*
> *You see, me and my homeys like to play this game.*
> *We call it Amtrack, but some call it the "train."*
> *We would all line up in a single file line,*
> *And take all our turns waxin' girls' behinds.*

Luther Campbell, lead singer of 2 Live Crew, in his autobiography, threatened to write a song about one of their favorite activities with groupies who came to their hotel after their concerts. After he and his "homeboys" have sex with their compliant fans, they end the festivities by urinating on these young girls. The name of the song, he mused, would be "Yellow Rain."

After my brother Dan and I debated Luther Campbell on *The Sally Jessy Raphael Show*, we walked off the set and asked God to purify our minds from anything that sick, demented man said and asked God to disband that group. God answered. We haven't heard anything from 2 Live Crew in years.

"Girls—L.G.B.N.A.F."
Ice-T

> *Girls, let's get butt naked*
> *and f——,*
> *I mean real stupid and nasty,*
> *. . . my crew got to have it.*
> *And after they dog it,*
> *I autograph it. . . .*

"Mind of a Lunatic"
The Geto Boys

> *She's naked*
> *and I'm a peeping tom*
> *Her body's beautiful,*
> *so I'm thinking rape . . .*
> *Leaving out the house,*
> *got the b———ch by her mouth,*
> *dragged her back in,*
> *slammed her down on the couch. . . .*

We pray that God will spare America's teens from this onslaught of perversion!

R.E.M., known more for its sympathetic tunes about social issues, sometimes opts for the tantalizing line. Michael Stipe sings:

> *Make your money with a pretty face . . .*
> *Make it charged with controversy . . .*
> *I'm straight, I'm queer, I'm bi.*[22]

The biggest album of 1996 was Alanis Morissette's "Jagged Little Pill." Her number-one hit "You Oughta Know" is a hate letter to her ex-boyfriend in which she asks about his latest amour, "Is she perverted like me?" In an angry snarl she queries, "Are you thinking of me when you f——— her?"[23] And—Americans spent more money purchasing this album than Bill Clinton and Bob Dole spent on the 1996 presidential election combined.

Rolling Stone described her CD as "uncensored documentation of her psychosexual former Catholic-girl torments."[24]

She said, "I was active . . . sexual(ly) when I was younger . . . deviant." When asked if she had ever slept with a woman, her answer was: "I'm open." She told *Spin* magazine that her parents weren't fazed when they heard her refer to oral sex and other sex acts on stage.

With this kind of steady bombardment through all the media—television, movies, and music—how is it possible for most teens to consider virginity until marriage, let alone maintain such an ideal? Peer pressure is bad enough, but when their heroes and heroines are telling the youth culture how wonderful it is out of wedlock, what hope do they have to resist? A steady diet of music like this is a form of brainwashing. Somehow we must help to show them that much of rock music is not worth the time, trouble, or money.

The Devil's Music

Many rock musicians claim to have a fascination with satanism if not an outright belief in it. And they sing about it in their music.

Slayer's album "Reign in Blood" starts with "Auschwitz, the Meaning of Pain" and ends with "Reign in Blood." In the process they give a "speed listening course in satanism, death, and hell."[25] Here is a sample from two of their songs:

"Altar of Sacrifice"

> *Waiting the hour,*
> *destined to die,*
> *here on the table of hell.*
> *High priest awaiting,*
> *dagger in hand,*
> *spilling the pure virgin blood.*
> *Satan's slaughter,*
> *enter the realm of Satan.*

"Necrophiliac"

> *I feel the urge,*
> *the growing need*
> *to f—— this*
> *sinful corpse.*
> *My task's complete*
> *the b——ch's soul*
> *like raped*
> *in demonic lust.*

Black Sabbath, whose albums are still around, and who continue to be adulated as paragons of the dark side, use these lyrics in "Killing Yourself to Live":

> *You're wishing that*

the hands of doom
could take your mind away.
And you don't care if you see
again the light of day.

Iron Maiden explores mythology, clairvoyance, and demonic possession on "Seventh Son of a Seventh Son." In "Only the Good Die Young" a boy commits suicide, and his soul falls into the possession of the devil.[26]

Megadeth's song, "Liar":

Start trouble, spread pain.
Piss and venom in your veins.
Talk nasty, breathe fire
Smell rotten, you're a liar.
Sweat liquor, breathe snot,
Eat garbage, spit blood.
. . . Rot in hell, it's time, you know.
To your Master, off you go.

Grim Reaper features a song that ends like this:

See you in hell, my friend.
See you in hell, my friend.
See you in hell, my friend.
I'll see you in hell.

According to Dr. Paul King, medical director of the adolescent unit at Charter Lakeside Hospital in Memphis, Tennessee, drug use, hate, devil worship, mutilation, brutality, and suicide are buzz words in music by W.A.S.P., Megadeth, AC/DC, Dio, Metallica, Slayer, Iron Maiden, Mötley Crüe, and more. Chemically dependent teens told Dr. King that if he wanted to understand their world, he had to understand their music. He conducted a study of 470 adolescent patients and found that 60 percent of them designated heavy metal music as their musical choice. "They said the music was a very important influence in their lives. In fact, it was their new religion. The use of drugs and alcohol had erased any concept of God that these kids had, and it got replaced with this new religion—heavy metal music.

"Every kid wants to have a sense of esteem and power, and if I'm not going to get it in a pro-social way—school, home, church—then I'm going to get it in some other way. In the negative way."

As is evidenced by the above lyrics, some lyrics and performances desensitize impressionable youth to brutality. Personal tragedies such as rape and suicide are trivialized and even romanticized. Emphasis and approval are heaped on immediate gratification and greed. Violence is glorified. This isn't only confined to heavy metal music. Danzig on its album "Lucifuge" is obsessed with portraying brutal violence, death, and destruction, as well as sex with demons and twisted occult oracles.

Day-Glo Abortions (punk rock) has two albums, "Feed Us a Fetus" and "Here Today, Guano Tomorrow," that are filled with four-letter words and descriptions of sex, brutality, rape, murder, and suicide. Their band members are listed as Cretin, Couch Potato, and Jesus Bonehead.

Tori Amos pens her songs about eroticism, spiritual confusion, and a distaste for Christianity. "Father Lucifer" asks the devil, "How's your Jesus Christ hanging?" She spouts obscenities, hatred, and blasphemies. On her CD cover she is breast-feeding a pig.[27]

Seal, a performer with some spiritually uplifting songs, lamented these trends in rock today, saying, "I don't think I would like any of my children to be exposed to some of the lyrics certain artists see fit to express in music."[28]

In Proverbs it is written, "To fear the Lord is to hate evil; I hate pride and arrogance, evil behavior and perverse speech" (8:13). Surely God desires that we hate this outpouring of evil and stand against it. If we don't, we may find ourselves committing the crimes the lyrics beckon us to commit.

Notes

1. Ginia Bellafante, "Finding Trauma Next Door," *Time* (October 13, 1997):41.
2. According to *Parental Guidance*, the Pumpkins' music contains "Angst-ridden lines about a life devoid of purpose . . . strewn throughout. 'Pissant' combines anger and apathy. On 'Plume,' lead singer Billy Corgan moans, 'My boredom has outshined the sun.' 'La Dolly Vita' is a being, in the song, who grants wisdom and visions . . . The F word appears in several places."

3. *Parental Guidance*, May 1995.
4. *Revolution*, September 1995, 40. *Rolling Stone*, Summer, vol. 3.
5. *St. Paul Pioneer Press*, July 1994, E-3.
6. *Spin*, July 1995, 81.
7. *End-Time Digest*, August 1984.
8. Bob Larsen, *Satanism*, 207.
9. *Plugged In*, formerly known as *Parental Guidance*, is published by Focus on the Family. This monthly magazine is available by writing to: Focus on the Family, *Plugged In*, Colorado Springs, CO 80995.
10. *Plugged In*, 1:2.
11. *Parental Guidance*, March 1995.
12. *Hit Parader*, no. 306.
13. John Tardy, *Power Metal*, 3:12.
14. *Arizona Republic* (December 11, 1997).
15. *Plugged In*, 1:11, 4.
16. *Rolling Stone*, January 1995, 40.
17. Ibid.
18. *San Diego Union Tribune*, January 3.
19. *Why Knock Rock?*, 67.
20. Ibid.
21. *Spin*, 12:12, 25.
22. *Rolling Stone*, October 1994, 62.
23. *People*, 45:9.
24. *Rolling Stone*, no. 720.
25. *Spin* (September 1996):32.
26. *Hit Parader*, 47:287.
27. *Plugged In*, 1:3.
28. *Entertainment Weekly* (March 3, 1997).

CHAPTER THREE

Lifestyles

I ask teens in my live Rock Music Seminar's Multi-Media Presentation to complete this verse from Proverbs 13:20: "He who walks with wise men shall be wise, but a companion of fools shall be _____." In loud chorus they shout out, "foolish." I retort, "Wrong. The Bible says that if you hang around fools you will be "DESTROYED"! It is extremely important who we hang around, what music we listen to, and whose lifestyle we imitate lest we be destroyed.

Contrary to common thought, how a person lives his life is not his own business. God himself scrutinizes every life, writing down every thought, word, and deed in His "books" (Rev. 20:12). One day, each person will stand before Him and be judged for his or her "deeds in the flesh."

Until then, it is up to us to determine whether a person is worthy of our following, imitating, or revering by how he or she lives. Jesus told his disciples repeatedly that "by their fruit [actions] you will recognize them" (Matt. 7:20). No matter how wonderful a guy is at playing guitar, no matter how sweet and beautiful a vocalist's voice, corruption in a life is still corruption.

The last few decades have brought forth few significant role models. Those who do stand up to be counted are often cut down quickly by the media as liars, adulterers, thieves, and racists.

When it comes to rock music, as we have seen in chapter 2,

anything goes. Rock stars are applauded not only for their musical skills but for how many women they've seduced and how many drugs they've used. No one seems to care how they live their lives as long as their songs top the charts.

And yet Scripture admonishes us repeatedly to look at lifestyle to know the true depth of an individual. Therein we see both the reality and the lie. In Galatians, the apostle Paul contrasts two types of fruit—the fruit of the flesh and the fruit of the Spirit. "Now the deeds of the flesh are evident, which are: immorality, impurity, sensuality, idolatry, sorcery, enmities, strife, jealousy, outbursts of anger, disputes, dissensions, factions, envyings, drunkenness, carousings, and things like these, of which I forewarn you just as I have forewarned you that those who practice such things shall not inherit the kingdom of God" (5:19–21, NASB).

In contrast is the fruit of the Spirit: "love, joy, peace, patience, kindness, goodness, faithfulness, gentleness, self-control" (Gal. 5:22–23, NASB).

Promiscuity and Hedonism

One of the primary areas in which rock musicians fail to measure up to Scripture's standard is in the area of illicit sex—fornication, bisexuality, and homosexuality. Elton John, praised and lauded for his all-time best-selling tribute to Princess Diana, once said, "There's nothing wrong with going to bed with someone of your own sex. I just think people should be very free with sex. . . . They should draw the line at goats."[1] John has also admitted to using several kinds of drugs.

Such attitudes go hand in hand with what rock 'n' roll is all about. Traci Guns of L.A. Guns has been quoted as saying, "Sex, drugs, and rock . . . sure work wonders for me. I admit that I drink. . . . I f—— as many women as I can—and I do recommend [it]. Hey, it's all part of rock and roll."[2]

From a band member of Skid Row: "I'm not a role model for anyone. . . . Hey, I'm young and I'm horny. I'm not gonna tie myself down to one woman."[3]

The Spice Girls, whose single "Wannabe" climbed the charts in 1997, are a strange mix. *Time* magazine characterizes them this way: "There's Mel B., with her curly hair and pierced tongue; cool, unsmiling Victoria; Mel C., with her dark locks and sassy nose stud; red-haired Geri, of whom old topless photos have turned up in those naughty English tabs; and blond 'Baby Spice' Emma, who claimed to be 19 but recently held a rather indiscreet 21st birthday party."[4] MTV anointed them "Band of the Year" in 1997.

TLC, whose album "CrazySexyCool" sold in the millions, have been cited for their promiscuous outlook. *Rolling Stone* said of them, " 'Creep' describes the darker side of TLC's giddy hedonism [promiscuity] and belies their fashionable bad-girl image."[5] It has been suggested that these "female rappers [have succumbed] to erotic filth."[6] Their album contains "sex, sex, and more sex."[7]

And from Ani DiFranco: "I've never hidden, or skirted around any of the relationships I've had, be they with men, or women, or farm animals. Some people have a desperate need to put me in a box, but I don't identify as straight or gay."[8]

Rap musician D'Angelo said, "I'm trying to be as raw as I can be. I just want to make some real black music."[9]

At a time when teens need all the encouragement they can get to maintain sexual discipline and remain chaste until marriage, these rockers seem to be doing all they can to pull them into the same sexual swamp they're in themselves. Father James Connor, of Holy Trinity Church in Washington, D.C., said in *Newsweek*, "At the very least, rock is turning sex into something casual. It's as if society is encouraging its youngsters to get sexually involved."[10]

The first three marks of a "flesh-directed" lifestyle are "immorality, impurity, and sensuality," which rock musicians not only take as a norm but as a badge. Jon Bon Jovi said this about touring with his band: "We ate, drank, sexually abused as many women as we could and played rock and roll. . . . What more is there to life?" He rips his fans, saying they're mostly fools: "It's hard to believe that the majority of teens today are so shallow-minded. Our songs are about lust, not love."[11] Bon Jovi has sold over 40 million albums.[12]

Scripture tells us to "come out from them and be separate" (2

Cor. 6:17). The danger of not separating from them is to be drawn into the same lifestyle.

Drugs and Alcohol

Rock stars' promotion of themselves as sexual aficionados and wonders is only the beginning. It carries over into the arena of drugs and alcohol, as well. For example, the group Alice in Chains has been reported to "maintain an unhealthy obsession with drugs."[13]

Members of Dangerous Toys proudly claim their addiction to alcohol: "There's nothing else to do on the road, really. It's out of habit and boredom that we get drunk. The first thing you do after a show is have a drink to help replenish your energy. . . . Partying gets to be a crucial thing; you start drinking every night."

The lead singer of Sublime, Brad Nowell, died of a heroin overdose on May 25, 1997, in a San Francisco hotel room at the age of twenty-eight.[14] "Gaugh [a member of the band] had raided Nowell's [heroin] stash. When he woke hours later, he discovered he'd been joined by Nowell, now lying stiffly at his side. That was probably supposed to be me. . . ." he said.

David Lee Roth, sometime front man for Van Halen, admits that such things are simply a part of who they are: "If there is any integrity in rock music, it's that we sing about the way we actually live. . . ."[15]

What they sing of is lust, drugs, drunkenness, and all manner of hedonism. They haven't reckoned with God or with judgment. As the psalmist says, "The fool says in his heart, 'There is no God' " (Ps. 14:1). Are fools worthy of devotion, adulation, and imitation?

Lack of Peace, Happiness, and Joy

One of the primary signs of the emptiness of the rock lifestyle and outlook is the fact that so many rock musicians are unhappy with life. They are dissatisfied and always in search of more.

John Mellencamp loves to tout his "bad-boy image" in rock culture. At the same time, he has admitted a profound disenchantment with life. "When you get older . . . it's hard to be happy. I have never had a full good day since I was 21."[16] His songs are filled with anti-everything lyrics. Perhaps the humor he adds to them enables him to listen to them over and over.

Gene Simmons of the revived band KISS said of the constant themes of unhappiness and brokenness in alternative music, "Everybody's so . . . depressed about everything, and there's absolutely nothing to be depressed about. . . . My philosophy is: Any day above ground is a good day. Everybody should get a life and stop whining, especially white middle-class kids."[17] Simmons makes an important complaint, but his only alternative is to live for today. God says, "This very night your soul is required of you; and now who will own what you have prepared?" (Luke 12:20 NASB).

Art Alexakis, from the rock group Everclear, said in *Entertainment Today*, "I feel depressed every day. I suffer from chemical depression. . . . I grew up without a dad on a housing project doing drugs, and drugs changed my chemical makeup. I'll get really bad anxiety attacks, or I'll get drug flashbacks."[18]

Perhaps the worst case of lifestyle ennui and emptiness is that of Kurt Cobain, the revered lead singer and composer with the Seattle grunge group Nirvana. Courtney Love, his widow, has recently released a biography of their last days together. Cobain was loved and emulated by many teens, who responded to his dark lyrics and godlike personality with nothing less than worship and devotion. Cobain, however, was anything but godlike.

In the book, Love said that Kurt's addiction to heroin had increased, and though she forbade him to use it in their 1.5 million-dollar house in Seattle, she finally relented because he spent all his time at hotels shooting up. After an aborted European tour with the band in which Kurt lost his voice, he returned to Seattle. Kurt was taking the antidepressant drug Klonopin in addition to the heroin. The combination exacerbated his depression and paranoia. Poppy Z. Brite, the author of the biography, writes:

> As well as heroin and Klonopin, Kurt had started doing speed. Never a big bather, he stopped washing altogether. He didn't sleep for a week. He seemed to have gone over the edge; nothing he did

made sense. He dressed in hunting gear—boots, a heavy jacket, a cap with ear flaps—and roamed the house with a shotgun.

On March 18 [1994], Courtney called 911. Kurt had locked himself in the bathroom with a bunch of guns, and she was sure he was going to kill himself. The police confiscated four guns, twenty-five boxes of ammunition, and a bottle of pills. On March 25, in desperation, Courtney staged an intervention. Kurt's old friend Dylan Carson, bass player Kris Novoselic, guitarist Pat Smear, and three of Nirvana's managers came to the house and took turns talking to him for five hours. They threatened to abandon him, to fire him. Afterward, Courtney could see that the session hadn't worked. Kurt had just been waiting for them to shut up so he could go take drugs.[19]

Cobain shot himself in the head with a shotgun on April 5, 1994.

Everyone could see it coming. During a concert in Rome, just months before, he freaked out, climbed atop the speaker columns, and threatened to dive to his death onto the arena floor.

When journalists asked him about becoming the voice of his generation, he replied, "I'm just as confused as most people. I don't have the answers for anything. I don't want to be a f——ing spokesperson."[20] Yet American record producers set this suicidal drug addict up as a world-renowned hero of the '90's! What a travesty.

Many rock musicians make the same claim. They don't want to be anyone's hero. And yet they eat up the adulation and money rewards without a look back. Wealth, fame, and fan-worship, however, are never enough. They refuse to take responsibility for warping their listeners' minds with their x-rated, satanic, lewd, and degrading lyrics. They claim a First Amendment right to degrade women with their music, pervert teen minds with their videos, and spread the debauchery of their wicked lifestyles through their concerts! But Jesus said, "The thief comes only to steal and kill and destroy; I have come that they may have life, and have it to the full" (John 10:10). There is no joy, peace, or real satisfaction in life without Christ.

Punk rocker Iggy Pop reveals part of the reason for the druggie lifestyle: "The only thing I thought might kill me off was clean living. I thought, 'How am I going to listen to that horrible noise I make without a gram of coke and a couple of double Jack Daniels?' "[21]

Pop singer Boy George, now on the list of the disappeared and forgotten, said in *Rolling Stone*, "I think everybody takes drugs for the same reason. People do it to escape. A lot of performers are very insecure people, and part of the whole reason why we want fame is that we want to be loved. What you find is that when you reach that peak where you're supposed to be satisfied, you're feeling just as empty because nothing outside of yourself can make you feel whole."[22]

All the stories, however, do not end up facedown in dirt. Paloma McLardy describes how she was molested as a child of five or six by a relative and eventually moved into the punk rock scene after years of moving around aimlessly with no sense of meaning or worth. Her boyfriend became a singer with The Clash, a famous punk rock band, and she became a drummer for The Slits. Paloma changed her name to "Palmolive" and began writing many of the songs for the group. She said in *Decision* magazine,

> The words of the songs revealed much of the turmoil that was in my heart. Punk rock music was a great outlet for the hurt and the pain that I felt. But it lacked any answers or real satisfaction. After two abortions and two broken relationships, I couldn't mask my disappointment any longer.
>
> I remember vividly a concert that I played in with *The Raincoats*. As people were leaving the venue, I observed that they were drunk and that they had a sadness and a heaviness about them. "I'm helping to make them like that," I thought. I was disturbed and lonely. I didn't believe in the things that I had stood for.
>
> My heart was like a barren landscape. The novelty of being in crisis and writing about it had worn off. After six months with *The Raincoats*, I decided to quit.

Paloma became a Christian in 1985 under the witness of a Christian nurse in a community in England where Paloma took care of handicapped people. She says,

> I asked God for forgiveness, and it was as if something had

exploded in my heart. My hatred, my bitterness, my loneliness and my self-pity exploded in a thousand fragments. I felt an excitement that no drug had ever given me. When I burned all my books about witchcraft, I felt great. I had never felt such dignity before. God could see right through me, and he still loved me! I knew that with his help I could do anything that he wanted me to.[23]

Unfortunately, her testimony is rare. Few rockers ever find the meaning and hope they seek as they continue in drugs, wealth, fame, and adulation.

Tell Me What You Believe

Nothing reveals better what rockers live for than their own honest statements about what they believe. For instance, Terence Trent D'Arby sings on his album "Vibrator," "I don't believe in the existence of sin."[24] If he did believe in its existence, he might find the answer to it in the forgiveness of Christ.

More and more, rock musicians are communicating a firmly established belief in nihilism, the conviction that traditional values and beliefs are unfounded and that existence is senseless and useless. No purpose, no standards, no guidelines. Nothing can satisfy the inner longing that is in every individual.

The band Cinderella has a song, "Somebody Save Me," that expresses the attitude:

Well, everybody's got opinions,
But nobody's got the answers.
And the s—— you ate for breakfast—
Well, it'll only give ya cancer.
We're runnin' in a circle,
runnin' to the morning light.
And if ya ain't quite workable,
it's been one hell of a night.
Somebody save me.
Somebody save me.

Depeche Mode voices similar feelings on "Fly on the Windscreen—Final."

Death is everywhere.
There are flies on the windscreen.
For a start, reminding us
we could be torn apart
Tonight.

Then, in "Black Celebration" they sing:

Let's have a black celebration,
black celebration tonight.
To celebrate the fact
that we've seen the back
of another black day. . . .

Psychiatrist Paul King calls heavy metal music "the new religion. Alienated kids find illusions of power in the anti-social, anti-Christian messages."[25] He says that "Young fans sport pentagram necklaces, upside-down crosses, skull and Grim Reaper tattoos. Kids become totally absorbed . . . dress like and get their philosophy and beliefs from band members."

White Zombie spent two years pushing "La Sexorcisto: Devil Music Vol. 1." They ravaged clubs, ransacked arenas, and closed down beer gardens. Nonetheless, their album went platinum after Beavis and Butthead deemed them cool.

Hell American freak.
I am the crawling dead . . .
Say acid suicide freedom
of the blast.
Read the f——ing lies . . .

Imagine This

The ultimate expression of the emptiness of his generation was John Lennon. His song "Imagine," long touted as one of the great texts of his life's work is, if anything, a nod at nihilism. "Imagine there's no heaven. . . . No hell below us, above us only sky. Imagine all the people, living for today . . . nothing to kill or die for and no religion, too."

Think about those words for a moment. A world with no heaven is a dead-end world. This life is all there is. For someone like John Lennon, who died with an estate estimated at over $120 million, this life is full of material success. But for millions, if not billions, of others the hope of heaven is what enables them to face the troubles of today.

No hell means no consequences for your actions. Do anything you want. It doesn't matter. You'll never be punished anyway. Such a philosophy leads to a Nazi Germany, or anarchy, or both.

"Imagine all the people living for today. . . ." Isn't that the very problem that is destroying our culture as we speak—people living for the moment, with no care about the future, no thought about whom their actions might hurt or how many bodies they'll leave behind in the rubble?

"Nothing to kill or die for . . ." A life without convictions and beliefs is a worthless life, little more than that of an animal. In such a world, people would either be zombies or mass murderers. The frustration of nothing to live for makes life unbearable.

Lennon's world as depicted in "Imagine" is a sad, broken, empty world. The last few years of his life, Lennon was so ravaged by his habitual drug use that he hid like a scared mouse, holed-up in his Dakota apartment in New York.

Just Be Cool

If it is not nihilism, rockers seem to think that simply being "cool" is enough. Snoop Doggy Dogg, one of the most successful rappers in the business, was acquitted of murder in 1996. He said in *Spin*, "There ain't nothing a young man can do to prepare himself for the hell I've gone through. I'm living positive. I've been through jail. I've been through selling drugs. I've been shot at. But I'm just as cool as ever. I don't understand the big misperception that people feel I'm a villain or something—I'm no sort of roughness. I'm a smooth macadamian."[26]

Snoop seems to think that being cool is all a man needs to be, and there are many who agree with him. Real character is much more costly but also much more valuable to God. "Precious in the sight of the Lord is the death of his saints" (Ps. 116:15).

Sometimes these rockers even claim to be Christians while speaking and acting in ways that belies their declaration. The Artist, formerly known as Prince, often dedicates his concerts to the Lord, then goes on to play music that is lascivious, incestuous, and filthy.

Gangsta rapper Scarface said in *Entertainment Today*, "I'm definitely a Christian. And I definitely don't believe that we just formed. Motherf——er try to come up with this big bang theory. But they need to stop trying to cut God out of the picture. It ain't no f—— ing way that you can do it. I mean, you spinning on this ball in the middle of nowhere and you the only form of life for 100 light years or more. And motherf——er still questioning God?"[27]

Some rockers mistakenly invoke God as the authority for their behavior. Courtney Love put it this way: "I don't think God necessarily put us here to be sober all the time, but I also don't think he put us here to be junkies."[28]

Outrageous, Anti-Christian, "In-Your-Face" Attitudes

An anti-God, anti-Christian outlook is blatantly put on display by some rockers. *Rolling Stone* magazine named Marilyn Manson the best new artist of 1996. Writer Neil Strauss explained in the article why he believed Brian Warner [Manson's real name] ultimately became Marilyn Manson: "Brian Warner would probably never have become Marilyn Manson if his parents hadn't sent him away to a private Christian school in 1974. It was there that he learned to deceive and manipulate the system."[29] Manson is as outrageous as possible and claims to be the antichrist, using sacrilegious lyrics.

Charles "Big Chick" Huntsberry, six feet six, 340 pounds, spent a long time in the '70s and '80s as a security guard and bouncer at concerts for Madonna, Nazareth, Iron Maiden, and others. He was personal bodyguard for Bon Scott of AC/DC for three years, and then for Prince for three and a half years. At one point in his life he had a $1,000-a-day cocaine habit. But in 1987, when his grandson was miraculously brought back from death after a choking incident, he rededicated his life to the Lord. He died of a heart attack in 1990. Steve Peters interviewed him in 1989 about his experiences in rock 'n' roll. Chick saw the hateful attitudes of many rockers traced back to the drugs they used.

"Drugs change you into something I can't explain. Drugs will make you do things that you don't want to do. One time I went on a roadies' bus and there was a young girl who'd been on there three or four days. She was tied up and naked and begging for water. I looked at her and said, 'What is this?' They said, 'Go back and do whatever you want to her. She's a piece of meat. She'll give you anything you want. Go back and use her.'"[30]

It is a vile, godless outlook that breeds the songs these bands produce.

Freddie Mercury, of the group Queen, died of AIDS as a result of his bisexual lifestyle. The movie *Wayne's World* gave Queen another breath of life as the characters sang along with "Bohemian Rhapsody" during one of their escapades. Roger Taylor, one of the band members, spoke of how frequently Mercury and the others used to enjoy watching nude female mud wrestlers and topless waitresses during their tours. "This is what Rock 'n' Roll is all about," he said, then added in another interview that he likes "strippers and wild parties with naked women. I'd love to own a whorehouse. What a wonderful way to make a living."[31]

Madonna's "Blonde Ambition" tour featured mimed masturbation during the song "Like A Virgin," and topless guys in foot-long point brassieres.[32] She said, "As long as I'm riding high on the charts, I don't care if they call me trashy or a slut. I'm proud of my image."

Bon Jovi became one of the favorite rock bands of the early '90s. Jon Bon Jovi, lead singer, pranced around on stage in black Spandex, and the girls threw garters, training bras, and notes onto the stage. He said if he had a week to live, he'd "stay drunk, eat like a pig, and sexually abuse as many women as I could get my hands on."[33]

He added, "I'll never be satisfied. I'm not happy to have the number one album, single, CD, video, that I sold out every show and that I fly in my airplane and that I can buy a huge mansion if I want to. . . . I want a bigger record. . . . I want to be able to buy two homes instead of one."

Beyond this is the anger and the rebellion that so many rockers promote. Mike Muir, lead singer of Suicidal Tendencies, said, "Hate can be a good thing if you let it . . . and I let it. Hate is to motivation what gasoline is to the engine."[34]

Mia Tyler, sixteen-year-old daughter of Aerosmith's Steven Tyler, talking on *A Current Affair* about her dad's onstage antics, said, "He stands there, and he's groping himself, and he is 46 years old and should not be doing that."[35]

Rapper Snoop Doggy Dogg is a hero to millions of kids. He sings of b——ches and "ho's," glorifies violence, admits he's sold drugs, and "smokes weed like a motherf——er."[36] His sex-and-violence-laden latest release, "Tha Doggfather" (Death Row Records) includes "Groupie," in which one man is instructed to "slap this b—ch;" "Downtown Assassins," which peeks into the world of drug dealing; and "Ride 4 Me," in which Snoop tells a fellow to shoot a rival.

The Fugees use "constant profanity" and "glorify violence, robbery, threats against police, gang shootings, assassinations, marijuana, whiskey, and murder."[37]

Ice-T admits, "I have a morbid fascination with violent actions . . . so lyrics like 'Shoot you in your face' turn me on. Is that wrong?"[38]

Worse than all this is the violent actions that many groups rely on to make news. One commentator said of Guns N' Roses that they're "hard-driving, hard-drinking, bad boys, who drink whiskey in huge amounts, destroy clubs, hold gang rapes in drunken orgies, and trash hotel rooms."

The Influence on Fans

Many question whether rock really has an influence on people. "It's benign," they say, "useless fluff. Entertainment." But the truth shows the lie behind such an attitude. When Jonathan Melvoin of Smashing Pumpkins died of a heroin overdose, the substance he died from, Red Rum, or "Mur-der" spelled backward, suddenly became a sought-after drug.

"It's kind of sick," says a commander of Manhattan's Downtown Narcotics District. "When people die from something or nearly die, all of a sudden there's this rush to get it because it must be more powerful and deliver a better high."[39]

Rapper LL Cool J said in *Rolling Stone* what he lets his children listen to: "I have records of my own I won't let them listen to. I'm an adult. I have a right to make the kind of music I want to make. At the same time, I have a responsibility to think about kids, too."[40] Unfortunately, he doesn't have the concern for other people's children that he has for his own.

When Robbie Williams quit the pop band Take That, German teenagers went crazy. After a fourteen-year-old girl attempted suicide, the Berlin government set up a telephone hotline. Distraught girls all over Germany called and asked for help.

"In Munich, four lines were set up to cope with distressed teenyboppers. More than 1,000 anguished calls were received on the youth program at Hamburg's North German Radio.

" 'One can best understand the emotional state of these girls, if one were to imagine Robbie Williams' departure from the band as the death of a close relative,' says a Berlin youth official. 'Callers exhibited acute pain, fury, and disappointment, as well as grave emotional distress,' she said."[41]

Frequently, radio stations offer raffles and crude contests whose prize is to meet their favorite rock stars. One of the most appalling happened in Texas where kids were asked to respond to the question, "What would you do to meet Mötley Crüe?" Here were several of the replies:

From a sixteen-year-old girl: "I would tie you up, spread-eagle and naked, with leather straps. Then I'd shave all the hair off your chest, and if I should nick you, I'll suck up all the blood as it slowly trickles over your body. . . ."

A thirteen-year-old said she'd "do it with Crüe till black and blue is all you see."

A nineteen-year-old said she "would go down to the local hardware store and buy some chains, leather straps, and nails. I would then put together the most outlandish outfit made of nothing but the leather straps, chains and nails. I'd go to the concert like this. . . . P.S. I would take a hammer so the guys [the Crüe] can loosen the nails off my outfit."

Some studies suggest that the average teen listens to 10,500 hours of rock music between seventh and twelfth grades. Thus, it should come as no surprise that this kind of response is the norm. Music surpasses television as an influence in a teen's life.

Christian musicians like Petra's lead singer John Schlitt recognize the power of this music and advise pastors and youth leaders not to "sit back waiting for kids to come to your meetings—you have to reach out. They'll gladly come once you have become part of their lives, but you have to make the first move.

"Music is a second language to teens today. Their taste in music identifies what kind of person they will be and even the style of clothes they will wear. If we don't understand how influential music is today, we will be missing out on some incredible ways to reach the coming generation. . . .

"This is a media generation, and teens expect fast-paced, visually stimulating programs. If you don't offer this, you risk losing them. . . . Be current, be cool, but make sure the music in your cool life is based on the Bible. . . ."[42]

Jesse Jackson, a spokesman for many African-Americans today, and who at times has vied to become president of the United States, said, "Our children's minds are being adversely affected and there is a definite correlation between the rising rate of illegitimacy and increasing numbers of abortions and songs about sex."[43]

We are not saying here that all rock music is rank evil. The key is to be discerning. What lyrics are we allowing to enter into our minds and the minds of our children? Seek God's wisdom for every kind of music you listen to. Anything less is foolish and irresponsible.

Notes

1. *Rolling Stone* (October 7, 1976):17.
2. *Hit Parader*, no. 306.

3. Ibid., no. 310.
4. Christopher John Farley, "New Girls on the Block," *Time* (February 3, 1997):68.
5. *Rolling Stone*, no. 715.
6. *Parental Guidance*, 9501.
7. *Rolling Stone*, no. 715.
8. *Entertainment Today* (September 1996).
9. *Vibe*, 3:5.
10. *Newsweek* (May 6, 1985).
11. *Cream Close-Up*, March 1985, RMR.
12. *Hit Parader*, no. 372.
13. *Parental Guidance*, September 1994.
14. *Spin*, 12:10.
15. ABC *Nightline* with Ted Koppel, debating the Peters Brothers.
16. *Why Knock Rock?*, 81.
17. *Wichita Eagle*, May 9, 1997.
18. *Entertainment Today* (September 3, 1997).
19. "Till Death Them Did Part," *People* magazine (September 1, 1997):128.
20. *Rolling Stone*, no. 628.
21. *Chicago Tribune*, October 24, 1996.
22. *Rolling Stone* (November 2, 1996).
23. Paloma McLardy, "From Punk Rock to Jesus," *Decision* magazine (August 1997):4–5.
24. *Vibe*, 3:5.
25. *USA Today*, August 18, 1986.
26. *Spin* (January 1997).
27. *Entertainment Today* (April 29, 1997).
28. *Rolling Stone* (July 31, 1997).
29. *Rolling Stone* (January 23, 1997).
30. From the cassette, "Sex, Violence, and Rock: Backstage with Rock's Meanest Bodyguard," by Steve Peters.
31. *Why Knock Rock?*, 80.
32. *People*, 33:18.
33. *RIP* magazine.
34. *Entertainment Today* (October 15, 1996).
35. *TV Guide* (January 21, 1997).
36. *Spin*, 12:11, 46.
37. Ibid.
38. *US* magazine, 1091–96.
39. *Pittsburgh Post-Gazette*, July 16.
40. *Rolling Stone* (June 27, 1997).
41. *Reuter/Variety* (July 25, 1997).
42. *Ministries Today* (September/October 1995).
43, *Why Knock Rock?*, 90.

CHAPTER FOUR

The Goals of Rock

Seventeen-year-old Ronald Clements was recently tried for the murder of a nineteen-year-old boy whom he and two of his friends beat to death with baseball bats. They weighted the body and dumped it into ten feet of water. Clements told psychiatrists that he had been inspired by a magazine interview with a heavy-metal star.

Clements sobbed in the courtroom as Megadeth's song "Good Morning, Black Friday" was played.

> *Killer, intruder, homicidal man,*
> *If you see me coming, run as fast as you can.*
> *A bloodthirsty demon who's stalking the street,*
> *I hack up my victims like pieces of meat.*

C. R. Rhoades, Clements's attorney, said the three boys, deeply involved in heavy-metal music, "thought they would somehow be rewarded by Satan."

When a performer makes a statement like the quote above, he is not only being irresponsible, but he is also subtly influencing young people to go and do likewise. In recent years, the world has seen many of these kinds of alleged results of rock 'n' roll music listening. These tragedies are no longer a rarity.

In Plano, Texas, Bruce and Bill, best friends, listened to the Pink Floyd album "Pink Floyd—The Wall," about a rock singer who builds a wall around his life to shut out the world. The two teens began dressing in rebel-style leather jackets and boots. One night, during a drag race, Bill was sideswiped accidentally and killed. Bruce kept to himself afterward, telling friends that he would see Bill again "some sunny day," a line from the album. The day after Bill's funeral, Bruce was found dead in his car of carbon monoxide poisoning. The cassette in the tape player was spun down to one of Pink Floyd's songs: "Goodbye, Cruel World."

Six days later another boy in Plano killed himself by the same method. According to *Newsweek*[1], his radio was blaring the same type of music.

Shofar magazine[2] reported that a young man committed suicide after listening to John Lennon's tune "Cold Turkey," about the horror of trying to quit drugs. Though the song didn't talk about suicide, the dark, pained lyrics could easily have added to his depression.

Steve Boucher, a quiet, sensitive kid, became a fan of KISS in 1978. In time, he developed an interest in AC/DC, as well. His bedroom walls were covered with their posters. Soon he began smoking marijuana. At the age of fourteen, Steve propped an inherited hunting rifle against his forehead and pulled the trigger.[3] Later, searching for clues as to why their son would take this tragic step, his parents began listening to his music. His mother said, "The one [song] that stands out in my mind the most is the AC/DC song 'Shoot to Thrill.'" It goes like this:

> *Are you willing?*
> *Keep it coming*
> *and put your head up to me.*
> *I'm gonna pull it, pull it,*
> *pull the trigger.*
> *Super thrill, way to kill . . .*
> *I've got my gun and I'm ready*
> *and I'm gonna fire at will.*

Other songs Steve loved about death and suicide were pounded into his mind until he finally did what the lyrics urged. Steve's father said, "[The music] gives suicide credibility—it promotes it, encourages it, advertises it."[4]

Another youth, John Tanner, tried to commit suicide with a shotgun, but the blast destroyed his face without killing him. He said, "I just lost my sense of worth through listening to a lot of acid rock and smoking pot. . . . I didn't really appreciate anything anymore. I started looking at the negative side of things. It just built up inside me."[5] John listened to albums by Black Sabbath, Grand Funk Railroad, and Blue Cheer constantly.

Ozzy Osbourne's "Suicide Solution":

Wine is fine but whiskey's quicker.
Suicide is slow with liquor.
Take a bottle, drown your sorrows,
then it floods away tomorrows. . . .
Where to hide, suicide is the only way out.

While few rock stars would ever claim that they promote teens killing themselves, the lyrics to their songs and their public statements prove otherwise.

What are the true goals of rock musicians? What do they want to promote in their music and lifestyle? The answers are little short of astonishing.

Let Me Outta Here

Spencer Dryden of Jefferson Starship, later Starship, once said his purpose was to "get them while they're young and bend their minds." And Frank Zappa, now deceased, explained the power of rock music on the mind: "I realized that this music got through to the youngsters because the big beat matched the great rhythms of the human body. And I further knew that they would carry this with them the rest of their lives."[6]

It's with such quotes in mind that we see the life-is-a-drag-so-let's-end-it-all message in much of rock's lyrics and music. If not that, it's the let's-run-away-to-where-life-is-beautiful-all-the-time trip, which is pure escapism. Rock musicians reflect the reality that is inside their own souls.

Green Day was named best new band by *Rolling Stone* readers and critics. *Rolling Stone* writer Chris Mundy says the trio gained the national spotlight because of their antics at Woodstock '94. Their third album, "Dookie," went double platinum, selling more than 3 million copies.

Mundy summarizes the album: "Embedded in the breakneck noise are lyrics that talk about mass destruction ('Having a Blast'), self-loathing and insanity ('Basket Case'), and hatred of the elder class ('Burnout'). It's a parent's nightmare. Which is, of course, a teenager's dream."

This is the sort of "nonsense" that produces the tragedies recorded earlier in this chapter.

The following are further quotes from *Rolling Stone's* interview with Chris Mundy:

At Woodstock II, Billie Joe Armstrong pulled down his pants and mooned the audience. He said, "[My mother] said that I was disrespectful and indecent and that if my father was alive, he would be ashamed of me. She couldn't believe I pulled my pants down and got in a fight on stage."

He also said, "I'm not going to say that I don't want to be a rock star. If you don't want to be a rock star, then quit. . . . But if I was to do it again, I'd do it differently. I want to try to make sense of all this and not become a parody of myself. I never really thought that being obnoxious would get me to where I am now. When I play, I'm not a nice guy. You know when you get really drunk, and it's like this person inside you that wants to come out and be obnoxious? It's kind of the same thing. And then people like you for it." He smiles and shakes his head. "I don't get that."

Mike Dirnt added, "I think drinking and doing drugs are very important. . . . To me, everybody should drop acid at least once. Well, some people don't have the right personality for it. But it is important."

Tre Cool jumped in with, "If someone throws a bag of weed on stage, Billie Joe will watch to make sure we don't get all f——ed up on it, but I dive right in."

Among other things, rock is about alcohol, drugs, and escapism.

While imagination and creativity are wonderful gifts of our humanity, point blank escapism is unrealistic and foolish. The apostle Paul spoke to the Corinthians about "casting down imaginations and every high thing that exalteth itself against the knowledge of God . . . bringing into captivity every thought to the obedience of Christ"(2 Cor. 10:5, KJV). For imagination to be productive, it must be joined with truth and reality.

God's music is the music of the heart: "Speak to one another with psalms, hymns and spiritual songs. Sing and make music in your heart to the Lord . . ." (Eph. 5:19).

Out to Destroy the Family Unit

A second theme you see in the goals of these rockers is the destruction of the family. King Coffey of the Butthole Surfers said in *Entertainment Today*, "[The Butthole Surfers is] a really great punk rock name because the whole idea of rock 'n' roll is to offend your parents."[7]

Rob Stryker of White Zombie says, "We're from New York City, so the sleaze and dirt that people associate with us is real. . . . We're just trying to communicate some feelings of violence, anger, and hatred."

Of course, one of the worst illustrations of this outlook is the outrageous sensation Marilyn Manson. *Hit Parader* wrote, "[It's a] dangerous path this androgynous, outrageous, hell-bent performer [is on]. . . . His goal is to infuriate, pushing perversion."[8] Manson's "songs [are] filled with images of abused children, tortured souls, and abhorrent societies."

Manson himself is quoted as saying, "If somebody kills themselves because of our music, then that's one less stupid person in the world. . . ."[9] His message to parents: "Raise your kids, or I'll be raising them for you."[10]

Such words warn but also dismay. Why are such people given a "bully pulpit" with which to spill their garbage? These are the kinds of people that the psalmist spoke of when he said, "The fool says in his heart, 'There is no God' " (Ps. 14:1). Yet we crown these people with glory, honor, wealth, and fame and allow our children to decorate their bedrooms with their images. Such behavior will not be winked at by God.

Pretty Packages

Some of the deception of rock lies in the "pretty package" way of marketing their goods and influencing the world. Their messages are tied up in brightly orchestrated melodies and harmonies so that in some cases their corrupt, evil lyrics are barely detectable. This, of course, is a form of rank commercialism. Rock isn't just about sex, Satan, and sleaze. It's also about money.

Debbie Harry, one-time front woman for the mega-hit group Blondie, said, "The major goal of any entertainer is to become easily identifiable. You have to find your own personal twist and play it up. Once you've done that, you start to click, regardless of your product. It's a psychological approach to sales."[11]

Mercyful Fate's front man, King Diamond, regards his own beliefs as benign and helpful: "Satanism isn't dangerous at all . . . it's a sound life philosophy."[12]

The influence of such rock personalities is huge, and it moves young people to try what these "heroes" have espoused. Richard Ramirez, the "Night Stalker" killer in Los Angeles, had a pentagram on the palm of his hand. He wrote satanic graffiti on victims' walls and shouted, "Hail, Satan" when exiting court. He was obsessed with AC/DC's "Highway to Hell" album, featuring the song "Night Stalker." Dr. Paul King says of this and similar incidents, "This is not to say the music made them into killers, but in their insane, drug-crazed thinking they identified strongly with the lyrics of the songs." Why is this material so attractive? Dr. King says, "The attraction of heavy metal music is its message that a higher power controls the world, and that power is hate—often personified by Satan. Hopeless, troubled youngsters can sink their teeth into this philosophy, so they crank up the music, tattoo or carve in their body a symbol of Satan, and do drugs, all of which makes them feel powerful and in charge."

The B–52s are very open about their fascination with mysticism and astrology: "An astrologer I know said that the reason we work so well together is because of our signs," said member Keith Strickland, a Buddhist. Other bands talk about their devotion to Buddha, Allah, New Age philosophies, and more. But satanism seems to be the most common symbol in rock songs.

King Diamond said, "I believe in satanism. I'm 200 percent into it." In his live show he pretends to chop his mother in half. In "Cremation" he is burned in a coffin. "I profess to being a satanist. . . ." he says. "I understand the powers of the unknown."

USA Today reported that Satanic Metal Music "has been called a contributing influence in murders in New York, California, Washington, and elsewhere."[13]

Anti-Religion

The general anti-religion stance of many rockers also is noteworthy.

Elvis Presley. Presley was a great fan of Madame Blavatsky, and also of a book called *The Impersonal Life*, supposedly recording words directly from God to Joseph S. Brenner. You couldn't visit or come into Elvis's presence without that book being somewhere nearby.[14]

John Denver. Killed in a plane crash in 1997, John Denver practiced EST, yoga, and occult science. "Someday I'll be so complete," he said, "I won't even be human. I'll be God."[15]

Peter Criss. A member of KISS, Criss once told an interviewer with *Rolling Stone*, "I find myself evil. I believe in the devil as much as God. You can use either one to get things done."[16]

Chick Huntsberry. The former bouncer, quoted in chapter 3, said, "Why do young people go to these rock shows? Because it's their idol; it's their god, in other words. They love rock and roll. It's not good until you're high. That's what it's about. Drugs are at every concert."

Soundgarden: "F—— you, you forty-nothing piece of sh——. They think they are so f——ing special. The f——ing Catholic-refugee, ex-hippie . . . don't want to be reminded they are old and bald.

Admit it: you hit 40 or 50, and life's gone."[17]

Ozzy Osbourne: "The things I get away with on stage, I'd get arrested for if I did them at home."[18] He has been known to bite the heads off doves and bats, throw offal (pig guts) on the audience, and trample puppies on stage.

Proverbs 10:23 says, "A fool finds pleasure in evil conduct."

The Almighty S-E-X Symbols

Once you get beyond all the glitter and gloss, the one anthem that resounds through the halls of rockdom is sex. Many musicians are simply in it for the sex. Chick Huntsberry told us, "What do you think rock 'n' roll is? It ain't Sunday School. It's violence. It's drugs. It's sex."

Some rock bands revel in the idea that they're the most promiscuous guys around. From the group Poison: "We probably f——— more women than any band. . . . We're horrible sluts on the road with women. We're terrible."[19]

Lita Ford talked about one of her songs, "Big Gun," this way: "[It's] about my favorite part of a guy's (anatomy)."[20] "Listen, rock and roll ain't church. It's a nasty business. Kids . . . want aggression, anger, and sleaze—they want rebels."[21]

Mick Jagger, the lead singer for the oldest and the "world's greatest rock and roll band," the Rolling Stones, said, responding to a reporter's suggestion that touring is just about making money, "What about all the beer you can drink and the girls down in front? There's other things than money."[22]

KISS, which has sold over 75 million albums, "roared into town straight from the gates of hell. . . . Sex and music are the same thing . . . the idea of rock and roll is to get laid. . . ."[23]

Warrant reports that it is "the horniest band in America." They brag, "We've downed between fifteen and twenty-five thousand beers on tour."[24]

What do such attitudes teach? Not only what is inside the hearts of these rockers but that humans are nothing better than animals, that they can be exploited and then discarded like garbage. It says there is nothing private or permanent or precious.

Rock stars are not telling the truth about sex. They make it a numbers game, an animalistic act. This is a far cry from what God intended, which is a oneness, a unity with another human being in a lifetime commitment. This kind of oneness requires one to "leave his father and mother and be united to his wife, and they will become one flesh" (Gen. 2:24). Anything less is a mockery, like trading a bowl of stew for a whole inheritance.

If the goals and attitudes mentioned in this chapter are those of the rock groups named, we surely have the responsibility to warn our young people and to see that we are not supporting these musicians in any way. The minds and hearts of our youth are too precious to be contaminated by this filth. It is important to remember, too, that what we have reported here is only a small portion of the true depth of the evil in this genre.

In a subsequent chapter, we will point out some of the good things coming out of some rock groups. There *is* another side to this.

Notes

1. August 15, 1983.
2. Fall 1983.
3. March 27, 1981.
4. *Why Knock Rock?*, 157–159.
5. Ibid., 160.
6. Ibid., 100.
7. *Entertainment Today,* August 27, 1996.
8. *Hit Parader,* no. 385.
9. Ibid.; *RIP* (February 1995).
10. *Parental Guidance,* 5:9.
11. *Why Knock Rock?*, 104.
12. *Graffiti,* vol. 5.
13. *USA Today,* August 18, 1986.
14. *Why Knock Rock?*, 110.
15. Ibid.
16. Ibid., 111.
17. *Rolling Stone,* June 1994, 50.
18. *Hit Parader,* no. 306.

19. *Hit Parader*, 47:287.
20. Ibid., 49:311.
21. *L.A. Times*, Media Update, 9.
22. *Chicago Tribune*, January 1, 1997.
23. *Hit Parader*, no. 389.
24. *RIP*, no. 689; *Hit Parader*, no. 1189; *Spin*, no. 1189.

CHAPTER FIVE

Graphics and Packaging

The modern purveyors of pop, alternative, rockabilly, and all else musical know that a picture often sells an album. Packaging is paramount. Album covers are designed both to sell the album and to give a cameo view of what the album is about. But why do so many album covers, videos, and other rock paraphernalia promote sex, nihilism, meaninglessness, drugs, the bizarre, and the occult?

God has warned us repeatedly not to expose ourselves to evil things, words, practices, and deeds. Paul told Timothy to "flee the evil desires of youth." He warned the Thessalonians to "avoid every kind of evil." Can any Christian, in light of such straight commands, ignore God's will when it comes to the graphic materials produced in today's secular rock music market? How can we show hatred for sin when we have smut-covered albums stacked by our stereos?

When videos and graphics are designed, much effort and planning goes into them. Michael Jackson's videos for "Thriller" and "Beat It" reportedly cost millions of dollars. They're regarded as mini-movies. But they have a greater impact than the average movie because fans watch them over and over. A song from a movie can be remembered long after the plot is forgotten.

In the following pages, we will look at graphics being produced today. We can give only a small selection, but any visit to the music or video store will reveal that this smattering is not out of the ordinary. Remember also that albums often contain photos and graphics on the inside layouts of CDs and cassettes. At present, no organization or government group plays watchdog over what is produced in this market. As a result, nearly anything goes.

Read on with utmost concern and prayer.

Sexual, Nihilistic, and Occultic

The Black Crowes—"Three Snakes and One Charm"—on the cover is what appears to be some kind of occultic symbol made of three writhing snakes hooked to a central "charm." Columbia calls them a "rock and raunch" band.

Chemlab—"East Side Militia"—These "Machine-Rock" masters feature a hooded terrorist on the cover jamming a gun into the viewer's face. Columbia says their tunes range from the "chilling violent opener 'Exile on Mainline' to 'Pyromance'"—a romance with a pyromaniac?

TuTara—"Breaking the Ethers"—The album cover features a demonic-looking monster surrounded by strange (occultic?) symbols. Their music often comes with "Eastern-spiced raga rock."

Cowboy Mouth—"Are You With Me?"—The album cover looks up into the crotch of a clown in a jester costume with something dangling between his legs. We needn't ask what it's supposed to symbolize.

GWAR—"Carnival of Chaos"—This band thrashes and roars and spins tales of "blood, destruction, and killer penguins."

k.d. lang—"Drag"—The well-known lesbian appears in "drag" wearing a man's suit and slicked down hair, creating a definite male image. Lang's lesbianism is paraded throughout in her music.

Pink Floyd—"The Wall"—Still around since 1982 and selling strong. Cover features a man in the middle of a primal scream.

Morbid Angel—"Blessed are the Sick"—Death metal and "gloom and doom."

Dub War—"Pain"—Lead singer Benji screams and shrieks on this blend of thrash, metal, and hard-core punk.

Godflesh—"Songs of Love and Hate"—Album cover shows a crucified Christ in front of a dark city dreamscape.

These covers weren't selected for shock value. They are
included as a sample of what is currently available.
Many examples aren't fit to publish.

BAD RELIGION
Recipe for Hate

BONE THUGS-N-HARMONY
The Art of War

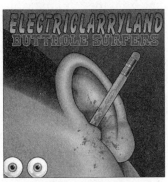

BUTTHOLE SURFERS
Electriclarryland

DECIDE
Serpents of the Light

GRAVEDIGGAZ
6 Feet Deep

MARILYN MANSON
Antichrist Superstar

These covers weren't selected for shock value. They are included as a sample of what is currently available. Many examples aren't fit to publish.

MARILYN MANSON
Portrait of an American Family

MINISTRY
Filth Pig

THE PRODIGY
Music For the Jilted Generation

RED HOT CHILI PEPPERS
Mother's Milk

SLAUGHTER
Fear No Evil

TOOL
Opiate

Fudge Tunnel—"Hate Songs in E Minor"—These noise-metal pioneers are said to chug out "chainsaw riffs, throbbing bass, and caustic lyrics."

Carcass—"Swansong"—The blurb reads, "Extreme death metal!!! Hell-spawned grind-core riffs, and themes of rotting flesh." Sound like fun?

At the Gates—"Slaughter of the Soul"—Another death-metal band in a malevolent mood.

Napalm Death—"Inside the Torn Apart"—This band is called the "godfathers of death metal." With a name like "Napalm Death" it definitely sounds like a fiery way to go.

KISS—"Kiss My A——: Classic KISS Regrooved"—The ultimate devil-rebel band's music still sells, and some of their fans are singing it, including Lenny Kravitz, Garth Brooks, the Gin Blossoms, and Anthrax.

Ghostface Killah—"Ironman"—This rapper throws plenty of "poisonous verbal darts" on such songs as "All That I Got Is You."

Marilyn Manson—"Antichrist Superstar"—His unalloyed satanic artistry is called by Columbia House a "masterpiece."

The above is just a sampling, but as you can see, the things that sell are raucous, rude, and raw. Even the names of some of the genres of music are revealing: thrash-metal, death-metal, and rage-metal.

Leaving the ads behind, let's look at some of the graphics a bit more closely. Among the many styles and pitches for attention we find the following:

Nudity and Illicit Sex

Michael Jackson appears nude on his "HIStory" video.

Nine Inch Nails' video "Closer" shows Trent Reznor's hands tied above his head. Contorted expression of pain pulsate. . . . Stripped to the waist, body writhing in agony and demented pleasure, he belts out, "I want to f—— you like an animal, I want to feel you from inside, my whole existence is flawed, you get me closer to God."

Dave Matthews Band's "Crash Into You" features the lyrics:

Hike up your skirt a little more
And show your world to me.

Hit Parader said of the band Pretty Boy Floyd, "They don't shoot from the hip—they shoot from the crotch. One look at the promotional postcard announcing their debut album makes this clear: the front flaunts living color photos of the four leather-clad members. The back is emblazoned with the suggestive legend 'Coming soon.' This band is a celebration of sleaze and glorious excess, a catharsis for teenage angst, rebellion, and newfound sexuality. If it's extreme, if it's flamboyant, if it's controversial, count on L.A.-based Pretty Boy Floyd to be doing it."

Danny Carey, drummer for the hard rock group Tool, said, "The video for 'Prison Sex' was the best one we have ever made, but it didn't get played nearly as much as 'Sober.' It's too bad. MTV played it for a little while but then said that too many kids were having nightmares, so they would only play it late at night. Personally, I like it when I have nightmares. I wake up and feel like I've accomplished something."[1]

Of the band 311, *Plugged In* says, "The band's name comes from a police code for indecent exposure, appropriate since young fans of this profane nonsense will be exposed to various forms of indecency. It's a musical frat party—pointless and puerile."[2] The band is a vocal supporter of NORML (the National Organization for the Reform of Marijuana Laws). They endorse drug abuse, perversity, obscenity, and reincarnation.

Madonna has defended the themes of unwed teen pregnancy, crotch grabbing, and sexual spanking. She toyed with voyeurism in "Open Your Heart," bondage in "Express Yourself," masturbation during the Blonde Ambition tour, and stigmata in "Like a Prayer." Her "Justify My Love" album was even banned by MTV! In this video she wore a black bra, stockings and heels, put the moves on a man, then kissed a woman dressed like a Nazi hooker with suspenders that barely covered her nipples. Bisexuality, homosexuality, lesbianism, and sado-masochism were all shown in a four-minute video.

Rolling Stone said of D Generation: "Working the crowd into a frenzy, Malin throws himself on the floor, destroys equipment, and whips out his penis. 'No Way Out' is a song about the desire to kill yourself."[3]

These kinds of raw graphic images do nothing to advance or help young people to grow into mature, content, and contributing adults. A study of 2,380 cases of abuse, battering, sexual assault, and exploitation found that "in 68 percent of the cases, the abuser beat or sexually abused the victim after looking at pornographic materials."[4]

Anti-Christianity

Most hard rockers deny charges that their music is evil or of the devil. But not Glen Danzig, singer for the band Danzig. *Entertainment Weekly* (October 14, 1996) reported his saying: "America was founded on satanism." His popular band released another album called "4."

MTV's standards and practices department rejected the video for the album's lead single, "Until You Call on the Dark," perhaps because of these blasphemous lyrics:

> *I wanna be the God who kills.*
> *I wanna be the Christ who dies*
> *Upon the fires of infamy.*

Danzig's response? "We're one of the only bands that get censored for theological commentary."

ET said, "But with fans like Beavis and Butthead—and thousands more like them—Danzig will scowl all the way to the bank, even if his satanism schtick is little more than a gag. 'Sometimes it's cynical,' he confesses of his public fascination with the occult. That fascination is broadening to include other violent imagery: he's formed a publishing company to produce adult comic books—one including a character named Satanika crossing lust with demonology. Like Danzig's other products, this is expected to appeal to the 'wispy-moustache set' with a passion for the lurid.

"Danzig doesn't consider himself as selling out to darker powers. 'If I were really in Satan's service, I would sweet-talk whoever I had to . . . to get my end result, and the dead bodies would be lying in piles everywhere.' "

MTV has been reported to show eighteen acts of violence in each hour of program time. Twenty-four percent of their viewing audience is age fourteen and under.[5] They influence movies, TV, drama, clothing, and lifestyles.[6]

Scripture tells us, "Do not be yoked together with unbelievers. For what do righteousness and wickedness have in common? Or what fellowship can light have with darkness?" (2 Cor. 6:14).

But how many of us allow our young people to watch cable stations like MTV for hours a day? Statisticians such as George Barna have produced research that shows the number of meaningful minutes per week parents spend with their teens: Moms spend less than thirty minutes; Dads less than fifteen minutes.[7] Yet kids pour many hours a day of rock music into their brains.

What is the influence of such graphics, videos, lyrics, and tunes? Chick Huntsberry told us: "The harder the rock got playing, the more I wanted to get high. And then you know what I wanted to do? I wanted to hit someone. I used to be with a motorcycle gang a long time and we called ourselves the Stompers. Before we would go to a gang fight, we would put on hard rock music, drink wine, and dance to it till we got ourselves into such a frenzy that we just wanted to kill."

God told the people of Hosea's day, "My people are destroyed from lack of knowledge. Because you have rejected knowledge, I will also reject you as my priests" (Hos. 4:6). What would he say to us?

Notes

1. *Night & Day* (October 17, 1996).
2. *Plugged In*, 1:10 (October 15, 1996):4.
3. *Rolling Stone*, no. 701, 19.

4. Dr. Sara Lee Johnson, Washington County, Minn., survey reported in N Area *AFA* report, 992.
5. *U.S. News and World Report*, 10:85.
6. *Prime Time Live*, ABC.
7. Barna Research Group, Glendale, Calif.

CHAPTER SIX

Concerts

If any one part of the rock scene is more hazardous to your health than any other, it's the concerts. In Knoxville, Tennessee, an eighteen-year-old woman was raped while hundreds of fans looked on, doing nothing but smoking their joints and popping their pills. "They were just like animals," she told a reporter later. "Everybody was smoking marijuana."[1] In Santa Ana, California,[2] a seventeen-year-old girl was raped during a concert at the Irvine Meadows Amphitheatre. More than fifty people were sitting nearby and did nothing to help her.

At a Who concert in Cincinnati, Ohio, eleven fans were asphyxiated as the crowd pressed to enter the stadium. Pete Townshend, lead guitarist for the Who, said, "We're not going to let a little thing like this stop us. . . . We had a tour to do. We're a rock 'n' roll band. You know we don't [expletive-deleted] around worrying about eleven people dying. . . . When you go on the road you put an armor around yourself."[3]

Robberies, rapes, car thefts, stabbings, gang fights, rioting—and even assaults upon fans by rock stars themselves—all occur frequently at rock concerts.

Chick Huntsberry told us, "What do you expect when you go to a concert where all this violence is? Here these kids are, they are drinking, doing drugs, carrying knives . . . that's the thing . . . roughness. When these little kids would come up to us and start doing things, we'd whip them. We'd beat them. Throw them out in the alley. One time at a concert we beat this dude up so bad and put him in the garbage dumpster and shut the lid. I'm telling you this is rock and roll."

A letter to the *Washington Post*[4] decried the kinds of things witnessed at a concert: "The Beastie Boys don't do concerts, they do orgies. In Memphis they used a giant inflatable penis during their song, 'Fight for your right to party.' In Columbus, Georgia, they invited the girls in the audience to bare their breasts and have sex with the members of the crew. They altered the lyrics to refer to oral sex. The Columbus Chief of Police, Jim Wetherington, said, 'The Beastie Boys rap music trio should have been arrested for indecent exposure and disorderly conduct.' "

The problem is that many bands actually promote the violence and rebellion witnessed at concerts. Mick Jagger of the Rolling Stones said, "The only performance that really makes it is one that achieves madness."

Security Guard Allan Fugate of Louisville, Kentucky, describes rock concerts he has worked as places where marijuana smoke casts a constant blue haze and where nudity, lewd behavior, and violence are commonplace. It's normal, he says, to collect twenty to thirty knives and guns from fans before they enter the arena.

"Peer pressure is a big thing at rock concerts," he says, "and if you get in an environment where there is no authority—and that's what a rock concert is, total absence of authority—you're going to see the worst behavior as a general rule. . . . I would not let my kids go to a rock concert because it's dangerous!"

Robert Brzozowski was considered a tough kid, but he didn't make it beyond his youth. A week before his eighteenth birthday, he was stabbed in the parking lot at an AC/DC concert and died two hours later in a Minnesota hospital. A fifteen-year-old youth was responsible. One of Brzozowski's friends said, "Things like this happen at concerts; they get out of control."

Tipper Gore, wife of Al Gore, and once on the staff of Parents Music Research Center, says the factors that produce violence at rap concerts are all too obvious. "You've got an audience filled with disillusioned kids—some of them using drugs or alcohol. There are obscenities and violence in the lyrics. The performers have a tough image and attitude. Finally, the rhythm gets them going, and makes some kids snap."

An AC/DC concert in Salt Lake City left three people crushed to death after 13,000 fans rushed the stage to get closer to the band. AC/DC made no comment on the tragedy. In fact, they simply kept on playing as paramedics lifted the bodies over the crowd to get help.

One of the big attractions at many concerts today is the mosh pit. In a cleared-out area in front of the band, audience members grab, thrust, twirl, and push anyone into the pit, preferably people they don't know. Paul Cruise of Despised explains it: "You see a big mosh pack, right, everyone's slamming into everyone. It does look violent, but if someone hits you too hard, you just go, 'Listen, buy me a beer.' They'll say it's sweet and you'll be mates by the end of the night."

It's the outrageous antics and wild stage designs that produce such tragedies. The musicians writhe about, grope themselves, leer, and grimace as if possessed by a hundred devils. Meanwhile, strobes and smoke machines create an eerie, ethereal, otherworldly effect to make you think this place is almost sacred, separated from time, a place and space where anything goes. The earsplitting music cranks everyone into a frenzy.

Look to the Stage

One of the ways in which rock bands control a crowd is by what the band is doing onstage—not only playing music but acting out a play in opera fashion.

The Red Hot Chili Peppers are well known for their x-rated onstage antics. They call their music "hardcore, bone-crunching, mayhem, psychedelic sex funk from heaven." They are known to strut onstage wearing nothing but socks over their genitalia. "The sock is something we do as a display of energy and freedom. It's always a tremendous rush to get out there and just be flappin' in the wind."

Anthony Kiedis, lead singer, was convicted of indecent exposure and sexual battery in 1990.

Ted Nugent, while playing the title cut from his LP "Little Miss Dangerous" at his concerts, lifted a willing groupie onstage, stripped off all but her garter belt and hose, and simulated sex on the drum stage. Though the girl was usually a plant, sometimes she had been a local teenage winner of a regional radio station contest.

The "Lovesexy" tour by Prince included such songs as "Erotic City," "I Wanna Be Your Lover," "Jack U Off," and "Head." With Cat, his onstage dirty dancer, Prince let her perform sexually erotic acts on a microphone between his legs.

Twiggy Ramirez, bandmate of Marilyn Manson, said about their concerts:

> "The cops made a big deal about a show where Marilyn [Manson] put some guy's d—— in his mouth onstage. But we've done much worse things than that. I had my eleven-year-old brother onstage in one of the shows completely naked. It was like child pornography."[5]

Madonna performed mimed masturbation in her "Like a Prayer" tour during her song "Like a Virgin." She told *People* magazine, "You all know the pleasures of a good spanking," referring to her song "Hanky Panky," an ode to the joy of the backside slap. Its lyrics say,

Some guys like to sweet talk,
Some guys like to tease,
Tie my hands behind my back
And I'm in ecstasy.

Gibby Haynes of the Butthole Surfers said, "It's really funny when I think of all the different moments when Kathleen [the lead singer] has been yanked off the stage. One time in Minneapolis there was a guy who got up on stage and had his d—— out and was j——ing off this limp d——. Kathleen was up there dancin' with her t——s way out and this guy was just there for a long time. Then after the show, they arrested Kathleen."[6]

Kids see these things go on, and what do they decide? It's cool. It's fun. It's right. Nobody should tell me I can't do it.

Bob Stewart and Dwight Silverman, staffers with the *San Antonio Light*, wrote, "If every parent in America attended just one heavy metal concert like the one we saw here last week, such goings-on would cease to exist. The crowd went wild over Iron Maiden, a heavy metal band. Several entertainers pranced on the stage with their leather pants cut out to expose their backsides. It was revolting."

The Audiences Are Nearly as Bad

Nonetheless, we can't put everything down as rock stars' excesses. The crowd joins in with similar lasciviousness and grossness. Ozzy Osbourne, one time notorious for his disgusting actions onstage, admitted he was usually drunk at the time and didn't remember what he'd done until someone told him the next day. "Some things, like when I bit the head off the bat, I do remember. But that was more of a mistake than anything else. Who would ever have imagined that the f——ing beast was actually alive? I thought it was some rubber toy that a kid threw onstage."

Steve Cisney of Akron, Ohio, a security guard at Cleveland Stadium and Blossom Music Center, a former bodyguard and bouncer for such '70s rock artists as the Eagles, Pink Floyd, and Elton John, comments on the things he'd see regularly at concerts: people shooting up heroin, smoking dope, drinking till drunk, urinating in public, performing open sex, starting fights, and carrying weapons. He remembers two women who traveled the country collecting the measurements of rock stars' genitalia to make plaster casts for a museum they intended to build.

"Everyone was living on the cutting edge," he says. "It was like holding a firecracker and waiting for it to explode. The groups were the fire that lit the fuse."

"The rock stars lived for the night. During the day they looked like walking skeletons. . . . There was no joy, no happiness. The crowd fed them their own glory. A rock guitarist once told me that they were lonely people, leading and directing a lot of other lonely people and no one knows where they're going."

Cisney became a Christian in the late '70s and works with young people, sometimes serving as security at Christian concerts where he rarely sees inappropriate behavior.

In the *Columbus Dispatch* it was reported that more than one hundred fifty of the city's police officers petitioned their superiors not to have to work heavy metal concerts any longer. At a Mötley Crüe concert in Tacoma, Washington, Detective Bill Belante said that during the concert he saw drug use, half-naked women, public sex, and, after a vicious beating, a young man licking spilled blood from the floor.

Warrant has a guitarist whose instrument is "like the packaging for a Trojan rubber," claims one band member, "and people are starting to throw rubbers up at him onstage. We're stocking up . . . on whatever we can get."

Paul Stanley, from KISS, proudly declared, "A couple of nights ago, this fabulous-looking girl took off all her clothes and threw them onstage . . . it wasn't anyone you'd ask to put them back on. Life on the road really has never changed—it is the ultimate buffet. It's just a matter of 'Do you want to eat?' "[7]

Chick Huntsberry said, "People want to hurt you at these concerts. They throw cherry bombs. It's like, if you've ever seen a shark: when the crowd starts, it's just like sharks going after blood. Kids go crazy. They just start running and they don't even know what they're doing. They'll do anything. They start hitting and ripping the clothes off."

The ultimate result of all this mayhem is that the music takes all the joy out of the good things in life and replaces them with lust, hatred, and other sinful actions.

What Do They Really Want?

What do many of these rock stars really want out of playing in concerts? Here are some quotes:

Bret Michaels of Poison said, "Every night after we're done playing, we spend an hour and a half in the dressing room, meeting the fans who come backstage. Then you meet a beautiful girl and an hour and a half turns into all night."[8]

Poison regards fun as "getting drunk every night and trashing hotel rooms, getting into fighting and screwing groupies, wanting to make a porno movie, traveling with a 'groupie computer,' and installing a condom machine on their tour bus." Michaels says "safe sex" is "not falling out of bed" while in the middle of intercourse. "We don't tell people how to live their lives and they shouldn't tell us how to live ours."[9]

W.A.S.P., which stands for, "We Are Sexual Perverts," simulate the torture of semi-nude women by throwing a girl up against a rack and pretending to rape and kill her, using a buzz-saw blade protruding from between the lead singer's legs.

The group Skid Row makes no apologies for its onstage outrages. Lead vocalist Sebastian "Baz" Bach has been arrested at least four times on obscenity charges —one time for leading his audience in shouting f—— one hundred times. In Fort Lauderdale, he encouraged women to take off their tops and lay their breasts on the stage.

Pamela Des Barres, an infamous rock groupie, said in her book *I'm With the Band*, "Something came over me in the presence of rock idols, something vile and despicable, something wondrous and holy." She says being with rock stars is a cross between "pornography and heaven."

"They're up there flaunting their stuff at you and the power of the music mingles with the passion and creates lust. I wanted to be the source of the music, the source of inciting that desire in me. . . . There's no such thing as casual lust, it can take over your life for a while. I'm sure some people ruin their entire lives over lust."[10]

Chick Huntsberry said, "I've seen girls come up to me and say, 'If you'll give me a backstage pass, I would do anything.' That's where the roadies come in. They are the ones who load in, load out all the stage material, sound equipment, everything. So, after they're all done, they don't have much to do. So they get backstage passes, and then the young girls come up and say, 'Hey, I'll do anything.' The roadies always say, 'I'm a personal friend of so and so, the big-shot, and I can get you personally back to talk to him. But you gotta take your clothes off. That's all you gotta do.' After he gets done with the girl, the line starts. Usually it ends up maybe fifteen or twenty guys. And these girls are so stupid they don't know what's going on."

This from Kreator, a heavy-metal band: "When we stand on stage and see hundreds of heads banging to our music or see people diving off the stage, we feel good. Those people are finding a release in our music. They may have come into the show full of anger and hostility toward a world that they feel is against them, but after our show they are relieved. Our music is almost a sexual thing to our fans and to us. We build to a great climax and then we all feel very happy and relieved."

In his book *The God of Rock*, Michael K. Haynes describes what he witnessed at a rock concert:

> The decibel level of the music was so loud that it shook the ground. The crowd was so worked up that they were hurting one another as well as themselves. The medics couldn't get to the ones who needed help; the beat was unbearable; the nudity was rampant; the drugs filled the air and the noses of the youth; the language was so vile it was an outright curse; the aid station was crowded with nice-looking young people who couldn't handle all or part of the above; and we had only gotten to the second act [Ozzy Osbourne]. . . .
>
> I thought of the reported deaths at this type of concert. I thought of the hospitalization . . . of the overdoses, the pregnancies, the illicit sex, the nudity, the outright punishment of human beings that I had witnessed. . . . Why is it that this has been going on for years and parents and churches are still in the dark? Either Satan is plenty shrewd, or we are just plain dumb.

This is indeed the question we are asking: How can we encourage or ignore this?

Notes

1. *Why Knock Rock?*, 177.
2. September 17, 1985.
3. *Why Knock Rock?*, 177.
4. V. H. Meyers, *Washington Post*, March 29, 1987.
5. *Entertainment Today*, January 7, 1997.

6. *Spin*, July 1990.

7. *Entertainment Today*, December 10, 1996.

8. *Hit Parader* (August 1990).

9. Ibid.

10. *I'm With the Band: The Confessions of a Groupie*, BeechTree Books, 1987. For a compendium of rock star indulgence, see Des Barres' latest book, *Rock Bottom: Dark Moments in Music Babylon*, St. Martin's Press, 1996.

CHAPTER SEVEN

Is There Anything Good About Rock and Roll Music?

In a book like this, one of the hardest elements is finding a balance point. We want to get across the fact that rock 'n' roll music, both as a genre and as a cultural arena, has serious problems. There are so few people in the media who will even deal with this issue that it is horrifying on the one hand and frustrating on the other.

When my brother Dan and I were on ABC's *Nightline*, Ted Koppel commented, "The media is all on the other side of this issue." He then turned to a First Amendment attorney (another guest on the show) and asked, "Just what are the Peters brothers supposed to do to bring the other side of the issue to light?"

Even Tipper Gore, who has spearheaded programs and committees committed to educating the public on the impurity of modern rock, has rarely received anything but a lukewarm welcome from the media. Few want to touch rock 'n' roll because many listen to it and enjoy it on some level. Your favorite artists probably seem pretty tame compared to some of the material you've found in this book. So what's the big deal?

That's part of the reason we've taken such a strong stand against rock. It doesn't mean we don't recognize that some good things can be found both in the people involved and in the music. Rock is not all evil. Nor are all rock musicians. Most musicians of long-standing have a few non-objectionable songs.

What are the good elements in rock that we can spotlight? We will try to do this in the material that follows.

Social Commentary

Rock musicians have often been on the cutting edge when it comes to social or cultural problems. Many unabashedly speak out against all manner of injustice, racism, hatred, nuclear weapons, and so on. Take Alanis Morissette, for instance. Her songs contain obscenities and psychosexual subject matter, but part of what makes her and her music popular is her passion and her rage at the way things are. In her hit "Ironic" she stresses how the worst things can happen just when you're on top of the world, like the man who wins the lottery and "dies the next day."

In "You Oughta Know" she talks about a lover who has left her behind with a huge mess. In the song, she cries out that she just wants him to know what he did to her. It's a plaintive cry of abject pain, something anyone can identify with who has been dumped in a dehumanizing way.

> And I'm here to remind you
> of the mess you left when you went away.
> It's not fair to deny you
> of the cross
> I bear that you gave to me.
> You you you oughta know.

In "You Learn" she croons,

> I recommend getting your heart
> trampled on to anyone,
> I recommend walking around naked
> in your living room.
> Swallow it down
> (what a jagged little pill).
> It feels so good
> (swimming in your stomach),

Then wait until the dust settles.
You live, you learn,
You love, you learn,
You cry, you learn,
You lose, you learn,
You bleed, you learn,
You scream, you learn.

The song speaks of the redemption in learning from pain. It may echo what living for Christ is all about, but Morissette doesn't offer the right answers. She only speaks powerfully to issues many feel in their very soul.

Don Henley, on his album "The End of the Innocence," talks about the end of a child's innocence when a father "had to fly." A family is left without a dad, and Henley decries the pain of that memory in these words:

Remember when the days were long
and we rode beneath the deep blue sky,
didn't have a care in the world
and Mommy and Daddy were standing by.
But happily ever after fails
and we've been poisoned by these fairy tales.
The lawyers dwell on small details
since Daddy had to fly.

On the same album, in a song called "The Heart of the Matter," Henley talks about a broken relationship that he wishes would heal. In the end, he finds the right answer to a hard question:

Been trying to get down
to the heart of the matter,
when everything changes
and my thoughts seem to scatter.
But I think it's about forgiveness,
forgiveness, even if, even if
you don't love me anymore.

There is something touching in these words. Henley, even if he isn't a Christian, has arrived at a salient, important point. He reminds us that the bedrock issue in many of our hurts is forgiveness.

Bruce Springsteen won an Oscar for his song "Streets of Philadelphia," which was the theme song for the movie *Philadelphia*. The movie is about a young homosexual lawyer who is diagnosed with AIDS and gets fired by his law firm. Christians readily admit the sinfulness of homosexuality. Some might even say that a homosexual who contracts AIDS is getting what he deserves. But if all of us were to get what we deserve . . . we'd be in deep trouble.

The portrait in the song is of a young man in deep pain. The music, muted and doleful, provides the perfect backdrop to what Springsteen is saying. The second and middle verses are heartbreaking:

> I walked the avenue
> till my legs felt like stone.
> I heard voices of friends,
> vanished and gone.
> At night I hear the blood in my veins,
> just as black and whispery as the rain,
> on the streets of Philadelphia.
> Ain't no angel gonna greet me.
> Just you and I, my friend.
> And my clothes don't fit me no more.
> I'd walk a thousand miles
> just to slip this skin.

Any sinner can identify with that kind of pain and horror. The consequences of sin (even though Springsteen doesn't call it that) are devastating, and the toll on human emotion in terms of hopelessness and despair is overwhelming. Springsteen has captured a certain grief and made us feel what it has done to one person. That's the power and beauty of song. I only wish Springsteen could have pointed his listeners to a solution.

Another light in the darkness is No Doubt's lead singer Gwen Stefani. *Details* magazine talked with her about a pro-choice organization that asked her to sing at a pro-choice benefit. During the concert she said, "If I got pregnant right now, I wouldn't get an abortion. But isn't it cool that nobody can tell me what I can and can't do." The pro-choice organization was appalled and miffed. They said she "wouldn't have played the gig if they'd known she was going to say that."[1]

While Stefani harbors no known Christian views, she used her platform for good. There is more reward for such things than this world can give, and that reward is the knowledge of doing right. It's something God puts into each of us.

U2's "Sunday Bloody Sunday," "MLK," and "Pride (In the Name of Love)" all speak of horrid crimes against humanity, the last song reminding us of the ultimate crime: Jesus' crucifixion.

Refreshment

A second way in which rock music with good lyrics may be helpful is simply through the relief it can bring after a long day. A melody with fragrant, uplifting words, can restore the soul. Some have found solace in Elton John's *Lion King* tune, "Can You Feel the Love Tonight?" Or his anthem to Marilyn Monroe, "Candle in the Wind," which was re-lyricked for his moving funeral ode to Princess Diana.

Others that may provide balm to the soul are Journey's song "Open Arms," the Doobie Brothers' "Listen to the Music," Kenny G's fine saxophone melodies, or the Beach Boys' "Kokomo." One feels lifted in spirit by good music.

In this respect, some in the secular rock arena bring an excellence to the medium. They know how to put together a good tune, even if they don't have the right answers.

Some Rock Musicians Have Honorable Intentions

To give credit where it is due, groups like Hootie and the Blowfish, a Columbia, South Carolina quartet, produce clean, easygoing rock 'n' roll.

"Everyone's getting sick of angry, aggressive rock," says band drummer Jim "Soni" Sonefeld. "We go down a little easier. We're safe."

The band's July 1994 debut album, "Cracked Rear View," was not expected to sell big. Surprise! Word of mouth propelled the album to 16 million in sales and many weeks atop the Billboard album charts.

"If anyone tells you we expected this, they're liars," says Val Azzoli, president of the band's label, Atlantic Records. "But these guys have hit a nerve. You know what? They're normal. . . . This country is looking for normality now—they're looking for heroes."

Band members hardly feel heroic, but Hootie appeals to people who loathe the nihilism of groups like Nirvana and Nine Inch Nails. "It's like seeing my buddies onstage," says Phil Hopkins, a student at Virginia Tech. "They're happy, and they want everyone else to be happy, too. If people want to be depressed, they should go see someone else."

Manager Tim Sommer says the band is a healthy antidote to modern rock. "We live in the age of mope rock. In the '80s and '90s, bands used grunge and nihilism as a pose. They wore it like '70s rockers wore hair spray. But I knew there was a niche out there for a band with great attitude."[2]

The problem is that such bands who consciously try to offer uplifting and even spiritual product are few and far between.

But they're not the only ones. U2 has been called the "good guys of rock and roll" because they forbid anyone in their entourage using groupies for sexual exploitation while they're on tour. They don't espouse drugs, and three members of the band claim to be born-again Christians.

Hanson, a teeny-bopper group, appeared out of nowhere from Tulsa, Oklahoma, and hit a nerve with young teens. Three members of one family, Isaac, Taylor, and Zack are all home-schooled. They've made the charts with several songs from their first album. One of them, "I Will Come to You," could be a song about Jesus' promise to walk with us through the dark valley:

When you have no light to guide you
And no one to walk beside you,
I will come to you, oh, I will come to you.
When the night is dark and stormy
You won't have to reach out for me,
I will come to you, oh, I will come to you.

Regardless of whether this song is about Christ or about a good friend, it's uplifting and worthy of an audience.

Right Questions, Wrong Answers

A fourth way in which some rock has redemptive value is that every now and then a group comes out with a song that asks the right questions. That doesn't mean the answers are always right, but at least the questions are good. Isn't that where most of us were before we became Christians? Someone has said that most rock musicians "are lost people searching for answers in a dark world."

Joan Osborne's song "One of Us" poses an important question:

What if God was one of us,
Just a slob like one of us,
Just a stranger on the bus
tryin' to find his way home?

The fact is that God was one of us. Not a slob and no stranger to anyone who will seek him. But the question "What if?" could open up a conversation that might yield truth to those who will seek an honest answer.

Several years ago Styx came out with a song that point blank asked, "Show Me the Way." The lyrics speak of someone who is confused, lost, broken:

Every night I say a prayer,
in hopes that there's a heaven. . . .
Take me to the river
and wash my illusions away.
Someone, show me the way.
Someone, show me the way.

This plaintive cry begs for the answer that can only be found in Jesus Christ, the way, the truth, and the life. It can also be a lesson for Christians who only "tell" the way rather than "show" it.

In 1986 U2 was the "hottest ticket in rock" with their Grammy-winning song "I Still Haven't Found What I'm Looking For." Bono, the lead singer, cries,

I believe in the kingdom come,
then all the colors will bleed into one.
But you know I'm still running.
You broke the bonds,
You loosed the chains,
You carried the cross,
And my shame. . . .
You know I believe it.

In the song, the composers admit they believe, but they "still haven't found what they're looking for." It's the plight of one who may believe in God but hasn't yet committed himself to Christ. Or the song of the Christian who longs for full redemption in glory when he sees Christ in his new creation, reigning and ruling forever.

These kinds of words express something all of us have felt and that is the greatness of their music.

Some Rock Musicians Become Christians

Over the years, there have been a number of rock musicians who have become Christians:

Alice Cooper
Des Dickerson (Prince)
Sheila E.
John Elefante (Kansas)
Mark Farner (Grand Funk Railroad)
Jeff Fenholt (Black Sabbath)
M.C. Hammer
Kerry Livgren (Kansas)
Barry McGuire
Leon Patillo (Santana)
Dan Peek (America)
Johnny Rivers
Run DMC
B. J. Thomas
Vanity (Denise Matthews)
Rick Wakeman (Yes)

There are many others as well. A very interesting example of this was reported in *Entertainment Weekly*. Branley Smith started out as the original drummer for Hootie and the Blowfish. But he left the band to become a youth pastor at Taylor's First Baptist Church. Now he is attending seminary. With Hootie selling more than 16 million albums to date, Smith could have been set for life. But he says, "There's nothing in this world that can match the riches that come from a relationship with Christ. For that reason alone, I would have quit Hootie a thousand times over."

When the old band invited him to perform with them on an "Unplugged" MTV concert, some suggested Smith would want to perform on stage again. In declining the invitation, he said, "I have peace about the past and trust that this is where God wants me to be. As long as I have Christ, there won't be any regrets."[3]

Smith's story is the story of many rock musicians. Rock became the catalyst that led them to Christ.

The Verdict Is Not Yet In

Whatever verdict you pronounce over rock music, remember this: We will all give an answer to Jesus Christ for the deeds done in this body on the earth. The reality is that God uses many avenues to win people away from Satan's clutches. Sometimes He may even use rock music. In the end, all truth is God's truth. If He chooses to use Satan's own weapons against him, that is His prerogative.

It is very difficult to write a chapter like this because I certainly do not want to give carte blanche approval of the musicians cited. There is probably some good in every rock artist because no one is completely void of good in their life.

Just about the time I think I've found a good-clean-acceptable secular musician or band, they blow it on their next album or tour. And if I have recommended them, suddenly I find myself scrambling to thousands of teens who know—I WAS WRONG.

Just because an artist sings a good song, it does not make him good. Kids like to inform me, "I know my favorite artist is bad, but he sings one good song," thinking this justifies listening to them. If a murderer kills someone, but gives his victim's money to the poor—is he good or bad? Obviously, the stolen donation does not excuse the brutal murder. Neither does a good song on an evil album justify the artist.

Secular artists often expose real social or spiritual problems, but they rarely have a solution. Occasionally, by singing about the problem, they can popularize the cause. I believe teens are looking for solutions, for answers to their situations in life. Rarely are those solutions found on TV, in the movies, in secular rock, or even from their friends. That is why I've dedicated my life to shattering the myth of harmless music and using that as an opportunity to introduce thousands to Christ.

For many years we have loudly recommended that parents steer their teens toward Christian contemporary music. Thirty years ago there was little or no alternative to the music of the world. But today there are hundreds of groups from which to choose. And that brings us to the next chapter.

Notes

1. *Entertainment Weekly* (April 15, 1997).
2. *Entertainment Weekly* (July 28, 1994).
3. *Entertainment Today* (July 16, 1997).

CHAPTER EIGHT

The Christian Music Alternative

We've looked at the horrors of much of secular rock music, but what is the alternative? Must we as Christians listen only to sacred hymns? Is there room for rock 'n' roll in a Christian sense?

Definitely. For those who aren't aware of the fact, there's a whole culture of Christian contemporary music available in most Christian book and music stores and also in many of the secular music stores.

The issue here is whether we should be investing our time and money in something that fails to exalt Jesus Christ and, in many ways, supports the enemies of His kingdom.

You may argue that secular rock music is simply entertainment, something to fill in the background. But that argument fails when you look at the lyrics, lifestyles, goals, and graphics of many rock musicians. To buy their albums, attend their concerts, wear T-shirts with their faces and names on them, or put their posters on our walls is supporting and encouraging them in their ungodly lifestyles.

How can we make wise and godly choices when it comes to music? What questions should we be asking ourselves about our music preferences?

Here are four questions to get you started:

1. Does the music I listen to promote Christian morals, values, and attitudes?

2. Does it lift up Jesus and exalt him as Lord and Savior?

3. Does it teach truth and spiritual wisdom?

4. Does it move me closer to the Lord, to worship and love him, or does it draw me away from him?

If you can't say the music you listen to does any of these things, why do you listen to it? Paul warned the Ephesians to "be very careful, then, how you live—not as unwise but as wise, making the most of every opportunity, because the days are evil" (Eph. 5:15–16). To fill our lives with evil words, pictures, and pastimes is clearly not fitting for a Christian who seeks to honor God in his or her life. It is, rather, catering to the devil and his kingdom.

The days are "evil," Paul says. Every day on this earth affords us opportunities to do evil things, to think evil thoughts. The world, the flesh, and the devil are more than able to derail our walk with Jesus. TV, magazines, music, movies, and books can all contribute to what we think about and value. They entertain. But to be entertained is not what life is all about.

Christian vocalist Dallas Holm said, "We are the most entertained society in the world, and our lives are so cluttered with meaningless, worthless things. People just indulge in so much of no value. . . . If we Christians would just listen to what these people [rock artists] are saying and listen to what their desires are . . . there is no question that we . . . should have nothing to do with it. . . . I don't think . . . you can listen to it and please the Lord or do yourself any good."[1]

Entertainment doesn't satisfy in the long run. You might enjoy listening to your music, but where does it leave you afterward? Stronger, uplifted, better able to cope with the problems of life?

In Jesus' day, entertainment was not the issue it is today, because it was not available in so many forms. But people were thirsty for something more, something lasting, something of value. Jesus' response was, "If anyone is thirsty, let him come to me and drink. Whoever believes in me, as the Scripture has said, streams of living water shall flow from within him" (John 7:37–38).

Jesus provides the answer to true spiritual thirst—the thirst for personal meaning and significance, for lasting joy and peace, the desire to love and to be loved. These are the things Jesus came to give. Much of secular rock music perverts and destroys these thirsts.

A good alternative to secular rock music is contemporary Christian music. A significant number of artists have recorded albums in every genre of modern music. These musicians are committed to exalting Jesus in their music. Their concerts are more like rousing worship services. The riffs, melodies, and lyrics they bring to the stage lift the heart and move us to love the Lord, love one another, and love the lost.

Christian rock guitarist and vocalist Phil Keaggy is sometimes listed with Eric Clapton, Stevie Ray Vaughan, and others, as one of the finest guitarists in the world. He has said, "In the context of a concert situation, the whole point is to lift up Jesus."[2] Keaggy's concerts become acts of worship, and create an emotional high of the soul that is far more beautiful and exciting than any rush one might get listening to Metallica, KORN, or Spice Girls.

During Christian rock concerts, the front man will often share his faith in a light, easygoing manner between songs. The setting is spiritual without any heavy church overtones. Kids come to the Lord, repent of their sins, and find new life when they hear these godly men and women perform. Christian music is about knowing God, about eternal life, not something that glimmers on the Top 40 for a few weeks and then disappears.

Of course, just because a band's album is sold in a Christian bookstore doesn't mean it is necessarily worth listening to. You must put Christian music to the same test as secular rock:

1. *What do the lyrics say?* Who or what is being exalted? Are the words edifying? Is the doctrine sound?

Christian musicians have a biblical responsibility that might be best exemplified by Paul's words to the Corinthians: "Whether you eat or drink or whatever you do, do it all for the glory of God" (1 Cor. 10:31). Anything that fails to exalt Christ, to build up your relationship with him or with others, is not worthwhile. Why give your time and money to things that have no eternal value?

2. *What about the lifestyles of the Christians performing the music?* In recent years several scandals have shattered the illusion that all Christian musicians are squeaky clean. Drugs and immorality have damaged both lives and careers. Find out who the musicians are that

you listen to and what they stand for by their lifestyles. If it looks like money and glitter, image and posturing are at the forefront, they might not be the best choice.

3. *What goals do these musicians espouse?* You can discover these in the lyrics or in articles written about the bands and performers. Some Christian musicians seem to be in it more for self-glorification and making big money than for any truly spiritual purpose.

4. *What do their album cover graphics show?* Are they in any way lascivious, raunchy, or sensual? For the most part, Christian CD covers are illustrative and seek to convey the message of the music. But when a so-called "star" uses his image and looks to flaunt his sexuality, something is amiss. The only real superstar in Christian music is Jesus. Everyone else is a servant.

Are these standards too high? We don't think so. God holds us to the standard of Jesus himself, and even if grace and forgiveness are the primary message of the gospel, the Lord is still in the business of making us like Jesus. Christian musicians should be growing in their faith and walk as much as any of their fans. In fact, James said that "we who teach will be judged more strictly" (James 3:1).

Changing Over Could Be Tough

If you give Christian music a chance, you may be surprised at the excellence and illumination that comes from listening to it. The transition could be tough, though. Secular rock music appeals strongly to the senses and the natural desires of the human heart, however depraved. So it will, in many ways, seem more appealing. But, like anything, tastes and habits are developed. Over time you will find Christian music to be far more satisfying and enjoyable.

What Do Your Parents Think?

Have your parents asked you to stop listening to secular rock music? Then you should obey them. The fifth commandment has never been revoked. It tells us: "Honor your father and mother." This not only means outward obedience but humble, honest obedience from the heart. Such compliance is not without blessing. The fifth commandment is the only one of the ten given to Moses that God issued with a promise attached: "that it may go well with you and that you may enjoy long life on the earth" (see also Eph. 6:1–3). God will bless you in ways you can't imagine.

If you would like to find some contemporary Christian artists whose music you can respect and enjoy, go to a local Christian bookstore and check out what's available. Many bookstores today have listening booths so that you can actually listen to an album before you buy it. You can also ask your Christian friends who they like; maybe borrow a copy before you buy those albums for yourself.

A second benefit of visiting the Christian bookstore will be to introduce you to other wholesome entertainment, from Christian fiction to books on spiritual living and devotional texts designed to help you grow. Many Christian bookstores feature a bulletin board where you can find out what Christian musicians may be performing in your area.

Here's a general listing of many of today's Christian artists who have a zeal for the Lord and musical talent as well:

Rock

Big Tent Revival	King's X	John Schlitt (for his
Blackball	Kenny Marks	solo efforts)
Greg Chaisson	Miss Angie	Rebecca St. James
Code of Ethics	Geoff Moore & the	Three Crosses
DeGarmo & Key	Distance	The Throes
Guardian	Nouveaux	Tony Vincent
Halo	Petra	The Waiting
Holy Soldier	PFR	White Heart

Alternative

Adam Again	Breakfast With Amy	Considering Lily
All Star United	Cædmon's Call	Crashdog
Applehead	Chatterbox	Curious Fools
Argyle Park	The Choir	Dakota Motor Co.
Audio Adrenaline	Circle of Dust	Danielson
Black Cherry Soda	Clash of Symbols	dc Talk
Blenderhead	The Clergy	Dig Hay Zoose

The Dime Store
   Prophets
eager
Eden Burning
Elder
Focused
Hocus Pick
Hoi Polloi
Iona
Jacob's Trouble
Sarah Jahn
Jars of Clay
Jan Krist
The Kry
Chris Lizotte
The Lost Dogs
Love Coma

Lust Control
Luxury
Sarah Masen
Riki Michelle
Julie Miller
Morella's Forest
The Newsboys
Nina
Nobody Special
No Laughing Matter
One Bad Pig
Ordained Fate
Painted Orange
Leslie Phillips
Plankeye
Plumb
poor old lu

The Prayer Chain
Raspberry Jam
Savior Machine
The Seventy Sevens
Sixpence None the
   Richer
Smalltown Poets
Sometime Sunday
Starflyer 59
The Supertones
third day
Michelle Tumes
Undercover
Vector
Villanelle
Wish for Eden
Yonderboy

Metal

Believer
The Blamed
Bloodshed
The Brave
Bride
Crashdog
Crimson Thorn
The Crucified
Deliverance
Detritus

Fell Venus
Global Wave System
Grammatrain
Living Sacrifice
Mortification
MxPx
Paramecium
Precious Death
Rez Band
Seventh Angel

Shout
Six Feet Deep
Tamplin
Testament
Tourniquet
Unashamed
Vengeance Rising
White Cross
X-Propagation
X-Sinner

Pop/Contemporary

Aaron Jeoffrey
Carolyn Arends
Susan Ashton
Avalon
Brian Barrett
Margaret Becker
Bob Bennett
Lisa Bevill
Brent Bourgeois
Kim Boyce
Scott Wesley Brown

Steve Camp
Bob Carlisle
Carmen
Bruce Carroll
Gary Chapman
Steven Curtis
   Chapman
Ashley Cleveland
Clay Crosse
Al Denson
Bryan Duncan

East to West
Chris Eaton
John Elefante
Jason and the G-Men
Jon Gibson
Gina
Amy Grant
Kim Hill
Cheri Keaggy
Phil Keaggy
Wes King

Jennifer Knapp
Crystal Lewis
David Meece
Cindy Morgan
Amy Morriss
Rich Mullins
Newsong
Nicole
Michael O' Brien

Out of Eden
Out of the Grey
Paul Overstreet
Charlie Peacock
Peter Penrose
Poor Baker's Dozen
Johnny Q. Public
Chris Rice
Michael W. Smith

Three Soul Cry
Pam Thum
Tammy Trent
Kathy Troccoli
Jaci Valesquez
Jeni Vanadeau
Matthew Ward
Wayne Watson
The Winans

Inspirational

Acappella
Oleta Adams
Yolanda Adams
Anointed
Ray Boltz
Michael Brooks
Michael Card
Commissioned
Andrae Crouch
Sarah Delane
Dino
Phil Driscoll
4Him
Kirk Franklin
Don Francisco
Billy and Sarah Gaines

The Gaither Vocal
   Band
Glad
Al Green
Keith Green
Steve Green
Larnelle Harris
Harvest
Annie Herring
Cissy Houston
Dennis Jernigan
Graham Kendrick
Ron Kenoly
L.P.G.
Babbie Mason
Marty McCall

Don Moen
Fernando Ortega
Twila Paris
Janet Paschall
Sandi Patty
Phillips, Craig & Dean
Point of Grace
Sierra
Russ Taff
Take 6
John Michael Talbot
Tuesday's Child
Virtue
Hezekiah Walker
Witness

Rap/Hip Hop/Dance/R&B

Apocalypse
Scott Blackwell
Eric Champion
Children of Israel
Christafari
Church of Rhythm
The CMC's
Dawkins and Dawkins
DBA
dc Talk (early
   recordings)
The Disco Saints
D.O.C.

Dynamic Twins
The Echoing Green
E.T.W.
Freedom of Soul
Barry G.
God'z Original Ganstas
The Gospel Ganstas
The Gotee Brothers
Grits
KIIS
LaMore
Maximillian
Mortal

OGG'Z
Preachas in tha Hood
Reality Check
Reggae Praise
RhythmSaints
S.F.C.
S.S.M.O.B.
Soul Tempo
T-Bone
WorldWide Message
   Tribe
YWFC

Note: This listing is not exhaustive—new bands rise to the surface daily. But this sampling will give you a good start on whom to try in the genres you already enjoy. Remember, too, we're not giving personal approval for all the bands on this list. You still need to measure these bands against the categories we have discussed in this book—lyrics, lifestyle, goals, graphics, and concerts. Then you will be a competent and faithful final judge of what you allow to enter your mind.

Notes

1. *Why Knock Rock?*, 215–216.
2. Ibid., 219.

CHAPTER NINE

For the Rock Music Fan

Right now Satan is waging a war for your heart. He employs many vehicles to snag it, and he's not particular about any one vehicle, so long as it grabs your mind, entrances your heart, and absconds with your soul.

David Crosby of Crosby, Stills, and Nash admitted early on that the purpose of his music was to do this very thing without mentioning the devil or Satan. "I figured the only thing to do was steal their kids. I still think it's the only thing to do. By saying that, I'm not talking about kidnapping. I'm just talking about changing young people's value systems, which removes them from their parents' world very effectively."[1]

Crosby admits to his defining motive and purpose as a musician: he's out to steal your heart and thus your life. Spencer Dryden of the now defunct Jefferson Starship put it this way: "Get them when they're young and bend their minds."[2]

Guitarist Craig Chaquico likens a rock concert to a church service: "Rock concerts are the churches of today. Music puts them on a spiritual plane. All music is God."[3]

The long-dead leader of the Doors, Jim Morrison, said, "I feel spiritual up there performing. Think of us as erotic politicians."[4] Morrison was renowned for his eroticism as a singer, composer, and musician, and was arrested and charged with indecent exposure during one concert.

Malcolm McLaren, manager of punk rock groups, summed the rock scene up in this way: "Rock 'n' roll is pagan and primitive, and very jungle, and that's how it should be! The moment it stops being these things, it's dead. . . . That's what rock 'n' roll is meant to be about, isn't it? . . . the true meaning of rock . . . is sex, subversion, and style."[5]

We could marshal a legion of quotes to support this point, but why belabor it? Rock musicians want to change your values, fill your mind with sex, subversion, and rebellion, and bring you to worship in the unholy temple of hedonism, immorality, pornography, and profanity. They want to replace whatever moral code you have with their agenda. When you examine the lyrics, lifestyles, goals, and graphics of many modern rock bands, you find the same strata: They want you to love them, honor them, follow them, and, in effect, worship them as the caretakers of a new world.

But they have no power to bring in any new world. All they can do is use the already existing one for their own ends.

What is the best response to this worldview? Jesus spoke to the issue when He said, "What comes out of the man is what makes him 'unclean.' For from within, out of men's hearts, come evil thoughts, sexual immorality, theft, murder, adultery, greed, malice, deceit, lewdness, envy, slander, arrogance and folly. All these evils come from inside and make a man 'unclean' " (Mark 7:20–23). The list isn't complete, but it covers many of the practices and habits of secular rock musicians. Examples of this lifestyle are clearly portrayed on their album covers, in their lyrics, and in what is said in interviews. This behavior is revolting to God and subject to His divine judgment.

These are strong words, but our investigation has uncovered this and more.

How does a secular rock musician's lifestyle affect yours? If you listen to a steady diet of his music, you will be brought down to his level. It is precisely the agenda of many of these musicians: to make you "twice the son of hell" they are. They have become the high priests of a religion that worships at the altar of Satan and his demons. Their concert halls, amphitheaters, and stadiums are the "churches." And their songs are the "prayers" of the faithful.

The question is, have you become such a worshiper? How can you know if you have? In what ways and to what degree do you imitate, support, and follow secular rock musicians and their bands?

Take a Simple Test

1. How much money do you spend on rock music, magazines, videos, stories, clothing, and other paraphernalia? In contrast, how much money do you spend building up the kingdom of God (donations to church, Christian ministries, missionaries, etc.)?

2. How much time do you spend listening to rock music on the radio, TV, your cassette or CD player? (Studies have shown that the national average is 6.3 hours a day). In contrast, how much time do you spend a day in prayer, in Bible study, in worship, or listening to music and TV shows that glorify God?

3. How much time do you spend talking about and fantasizing over your favorite musicians and bands? In contrast, how much time do you spend thinking about and talking about the things of God?

4. How many times do you get into conflict with your parents over your rock music preferences? In contrast, how often do you fight and argue about going to church, participating in Christian youth activities, and listening to Christian music?

We ask these questions not to shame or condemn you but simply to cause you to stop and think. Remember, a war rages around us to keep lost souls lost and Christians foundering in a sea of compromise and shallow living. Satan will do anything to destroy us. And, clearly, many performers in secular rock music today are his tools and henchmen.

But you may look at the questions above and say something like this: "How much time can you give to prayer and Bible study and going to church? It is difficult to do. Plus, rock music is just entertainment. I'm not worshiping anything or anyone."

When you devote many dollars each month to the purchase of rock music materials, spend hours a day participating in the lyrics and attitudes of the music itself, wear clothing that glorifies certain groups, and then think and talk about rock personalities several times a day, you are in essence "bowing the knee" to them, attributing worth to them. That, my friend, is a form of worship.

A good word from Isaiah says, "These people come near to me with their mouth and honor me with their lips, but their hearts are far from me. Their worship of me is made up only of rules taught by men. . . . Woe to those who go to great depths to hide their plans from the Lord, who do their works in darkness and think, 'Who sees us? Who will know?' " (29:13, 15).

God ultimately rejects words that are only that and worship that is only duty. He honors action. Those who go to church for an hour on Sunday but have little to do with the Lord the rest of the week will find Him far away when they need Him. Not because He doesn't care or cannot help, but because our hearts have departed so far from Him.

Gene Simmons, lead singer of the revived heavy metal band KISS, once said that we're on our own in this world to "make our own mistakes, to get ourselves out of trouble."[6]

Simmons was right in one way: Those who reject God are on their own. God makes no promises to them.

Jesus repeatedly told His disciples, "He who is not with me is against me, and he who does not gather with me scatters" (Matt. 12:30). What Jesus meant was that if you're not publicly and personally aligned with Him, you're actually fighting against Him and are part of the problem. If you're not working for His kingdom, you are by default causing it harm.

We are not telling you that you have to pray and read the Bible and attend church six hours a day. We are merely pointing out a staggering contrast. When the average teenager spends nearly six and a half hours a day listening to rock music, he is devoting a huge part of his day and his life to something that is at best mere entertainment and at worst satanic and evil. If Jesus said we will be judged by "every word we have spoken," don't you think that applies to words we have listened to and sung along with and praised?

All secular rock music is not evil and satanic. There are many

musicians whose purpose is to write an endearing love song or protest a societal wrong or simply give his or her listeners "a good time."
But there are far more who are lethally seeking our spiritual destruction.

What do we do? How do we respond?

You Can Be Free Indeed

Would you like to be free of the bondage of the rock music culture? The first thing to do is to make sure of your salvation. Scripture says, "Therefore, my brothers, be all the more eager to make
your calling and election sure. For if you do these things, you will
never fall, and you will receive a rich welcome into the eternal kingdom of our Lord and Savior Jesus Christ" (2 Peter 1:10–11).

Peter encourages us to examine ourselves, to be diligent, to
make certain that Jesus has called and chosen us to be His disciples.
By taking such an inventory, we insure that we will enter His eternal
kingdom.

How do you make certain of God's salvation in your life? Have
you admitted known sin, repented of it, and recognized your need
of a Savior?

If you haven't, take a hard look at your life. Jesus told His disciples that if they didn't believe He was the Son of God, they would
"die in their sins" (John 8:23). That means they would die and face
God in eternity with their sins literally spread out before Him. Because God is holy and just, He must decree judgment on a person
who is not protected by the blood of Jesus. The ultimate penalty of
rejecting Christ is eternal damnation and separation from God forever. That is what Scripture teaches.

If you don't know if you are a Christian, or a sinner in need of
a Savior, ask yourself a few questions:

Am I unhappy with my life?

Am I dissatisfied with the way my life is going?

Do I often feel guilty about things I've done and worry that I'll
be caught?

Do I hide from my parents certain activities that would shock them if they knew about them?

Do I fear death (not the process of dying, but the aftermath)?

Do I ever contemplate (and even carry out) desires to commit sexual sin, murder, hatred, or suicide?

If you can answer any of these questions with a yes, and you also know that you haven't accepted Jesus as your Savior and Lord, you can find the peace, love, and freedom that comes through a relationship with Christ by confessing and forsaking all sin and taking Him into your life as your Savior and Lord now.

Part of the reason secular rock music may have such a hold on you is because you've never experienced the grace and love of God in your life.

Nothing makes life more worth living than knowing and walking with the living Christ. He himself said, "I have come that they may have life, and have it to the full" (John 10:10). Jesus came to give us a quality of life—love, joy, peace, patience, kindness, goodness, gentleness, faithfulness, self-control (imagine if you could have all those things in your life today!)—and a quantity of life: eternal life. He wants to give us the real thing.

Secular rock musicians often talk about the glamour and "joy" of their lifestyles. But behind the sex, drugs, and violence, we find a very different picture. Many artists' songs speak of despair, hatred, alienation, suicide, and a longing for death. Are these the anthems of people who are truly enjoying life?

True abundant life simply can't happen apart from God because He is the source of it. It's like trying to quench your thirst with sand. Your body's thirst is built only to be satisfied with water. Sand will only intensify your thirst. Much of rock music is quenching real spiritual thirst with handfuls of sand. It will not get the job done.

Remember, God has no interest in imprisoning you. He doesn't want to cram you into some mold and make you do things you don't want to do. Rather, He wants to set you free and allow you to live up to your potential as a human being and as a child of God. He is in the business of liberating lost lives, not liquidating them. He wants to shower us with blessing upon blessing. But He can't do that when we have a wall of sin separating us from Him.

If you find yourself longing for a relationship with God through Jesus, then simply tell Him that now. This very minute. If you don't know what to say, then try this prayer:

> Dear Lord Jesus, I know that I'm a sinner, and that I need your forgiveness. Please forgive me and take my life and make me new. I want you to be my personal Savior and Lord. I turn from my old way of life and choose to serve you now. Thank you, Jesus. Amen.

If you prayed that prayer and meant it, you have just made the greatest decision of your life. You are now an heir of heaven, a brother or sister of Jesus, and an ambassador to your friends of the Good News. Jesus will free you from guilt as you confess and turn from sin, and He will fill your life with good things you can't even begin to imagine. Starting now He is running your life while at the same time giving you complete freedom to make decisions and to live out your choices. He will be with you in every trouble and lead you through every storm. So trust Him, talk to Him, and listen to Him every moment of the day.

The Exciting Road Ahead

Leaving the secular rock music scene and committing your life to a Christian walk does not mean everything in life will suddenly be easy and perfect. You may miss some of that old music. If you were addicted to some band or genre of music, you might want to find music in the Christian market that is a realistic substitute (see chapter 8). But that doesn't mean you shouldn't try. Also, remember that we're not saying you automatically have to discard every bit of secular rock music. Ask the Lord through the insight of the Holy Spirit to show you what you should listen to.

The crux of the issue is choices. What are your best options when it comes to rock music? Do the lyrics, lifestyles, goals, and graphics of your favorite performers exalt the wrong things: death, suicide, immorality, and drugs? If they do, you need to prayerfully consider whether that is the music you should continue to listen to and support as a Christian.

On the other hand, if you honestly can't find a moral hole in a secular band's values and attitudes, there's no reason to think you must excise them permanently from your life—the Bible encourages us to approve the things that are excellent. The issue is choosing what is best for your life as you learn and grow in Christ. As you immerse yourself in Bible study, prayer, fellowship with other Christians, and a new lifestyle, you may simply find most of what you used to listen to unappealing.

Like dead leaves in the spring, as the growth of spirituality rises, the crinkled brown leaves of last year are pushed off to make room for the new growth. In some cases, a clean, unequivocal break is necessary, especially when your involvement has become an addiction. Many times, though, your interest in it will simply "fade away."

Whatever promotes growth in Christ should be emphasized and nurtured. Anything that prevents it should be examined and discarded.

It's really your choice. We pray that you make the wise one.

Notes

1. *Why Knock Rock?*, 96.
2. Ibid., 100.
3. Ibid., 105.
4. Ibid., 107.
5. Ibid.
6. Ibid., 221.

CHAPTER TEN

For Parents

Parents face an incredible task in steering their children and teenagers clear of the influence of filthy lyrics, drug-advertising lifestyles, hedonistic goals, and pornographic illustrations or pictures. Our culture is saturated with these images. Kids must deal with a daily onslaught from peers to get involved in un-Christian and often immoral activities. Where do you start?

The first place is to be sure you are not displaying hypocritical behavior. A teenager can spot a hypocrite at a hundred paces. If you as a parent listen to lurid or immoral music of any genre (rock, pop, country, or even the "classics"), watch endless questionable TV and videos, or spend time touting your own unbiblical or un-Christlike favorites, you are not going to be effective in reaching today's teenager. Many parents send this message to their children: "Do as I say, not as I do." But it doesn't work. Kids want reality, and your example is paramount. As the famed missionary doctor Albert Schweitzer once said, "Example is not the main thing in life. It is the only thing."

Ask yourself these questions:

1. Have you bought into the modern world's emphasis on financial success and personal pleasure? If so, you are at odds with Jesus Christ, who said, "Seek first his kingdom and his righteousness, and all these things will be given to you as well" (Matt. 6:33).

2. Can you honestly say that Jesus would feel comfortable par-

ticipating with you in the daily activities of your life, especially entertainment venues such as music, TV, movies, and videos? If not, ask yourself why you are engaging in those activities. We can't pass on to our children what we don't possess ourselves.

3. Are you using any stimulants—tobacco, drugs, alcohol? You may need to rethink your use of these things, for they may be sending the opposite message from the one you want to send to your children.

4. Are you building the kind of relationship with your kids that makes your influence the primary one of their lives? Some studies have found that the average parent spends thirty-seven seconds a day with each of his or her children. If those same kids are spending six hours a day tuned to rock music and an additional three hours in front of the TV, what hope do you have of making any of your values and attitudes stick? Many children are being raised by the media, not by their parents.

Undoubtedly, if you are a Christian parent, you know these things already. The more important question for you is, "What can I do about rock music and its influence on my kids?" Let us offer several lines of approach.

1. *Get smart.* If you're thinking that most of rock is like the early Beatles, the Four Tops, or the Lovin' Spoonful, you're in for a big surprise. Rock music today is a wide-open, spread-out, crazy, mixed-up bag of everything from the light and easy lyrics of the group Hanson to the hate-filled rap of Tupac Shakur.

To get smart about rock today, you need to do a fact-finding tour. First, go to a music store and browse through the album covers. You'll see everything from the wildly whimsical to the wholly satanic. Notice the other customers browsing those same shelves. It may be surprising to see some as young as ten years old.

What else is for sale in this music store—lava lamps, strobe lights, drug paraphernalia? These items reflect the same thing many rock stars promote: drugs. With every visit to this store, teens will be told by what they see and read that "drugs are fun. Drugs are good. Have a good time while you're listening to this music."

Next stop is the library, bookstore, or a magazine rack frequented by teens. Flip through magazines like *Teen Beat, Rolling Stone, Circus, Musician*, and *Rock Scene*. What kinds of pictures do you see? What is glorified in the stories of these people? You will find unabashed sensuality, sexuality, and drug addicts posing half clothed. It's not just about long hair anymore. Or just relaxing and being cool. These teen idols are serious about their rebellion, their hatred, and their rejection of society's values.

Now turn on the music. Listen to the lyrics and read along with the printed sheet sold with the CD or tape. You will be astonished. It is important to note that if you listen to these same hits on the radio, you will miss the four-letter words and some of the drug and sexual innuendoes because the radio deejays cut them out or record over them so they don't violate federal laws against pornography on the airwaves.

Next, tune in to MTV, VH1, or one of the other music video television stations. Here you will see the latest music videos being produced, with everyone from Madonna and Michael Jackson to the new one-hit *wunderkinds*. Be prepared for a shock. You are seeing your teenager's world in its full-color antic variety and volume. This is where many of them spend their time, money, and devotion.

As a final stop, use their music to build a bridge between you and your teenager. Ask your teen to show you his or her own rock music collection. Don't be afraid to ask them to play you a questionable song or a song that they feel will not meet your approval. Without condemnation, simply listen to the sound and the lyrics, then look at the pictures on the tape or CD album covers. Do this without judgment but with a view to discussing intelligently what your children are exposing their minds and hearts to.

2. *Get involved.* Spending time with your kids can be an awesome responsibility. Work, career, a social and church life, and other interests crowd out the very ones that God considers our most important mission field: our own family. Taking the time to get to know and show your love for your kids is essential. Why should they listen to you and accept your values and spiritual leadership? Be sure that they are not doing this outwardly to appease you but

inwardly because they love and respect you. Values are "caught, not taught."

Once you've begun to build a real relationship with your teenagers, and they have begun to share with you the real issues in their own lives, then and only then is it fruitful to begin a family discussion about rock music.

What should you talk about?

Amy Stephens in a *Focus on the Family* article asks,

> Do you know what's going on in your teen's world? Do you know what he or she likes, and why? In order to help your child sort out the positive music from the negative, talk about album lyrics by discussing these questions:
>
> 1. Do the words of the song emphasize harmful consequences or actions?
>
> 2. Do the artist's words or actions promote immediate gratification?
>
> 3. Do the words promote courage, self-control, and good judgment?
>
> 4. Do they emphasize secrecy?
>
> 5. Are the words or actions based primarily on feelings?
>
> 6. Finally, "Would Jesus listen to this?" (This question should also be applied to movies and TV shows.)
>
> It won't work to tell your teen, "You can't listen to that music." Instead, suggest positive Christian alternatives.

3. *Get on your knees.* This final admonition is crucial. Only through prayer and a spirit centered on Christ can you win this battle. Remember that you are fighting "not against flesh and blood, but against the rulers, against the authorities, against the powers of this dark world and against the spiritual forces of evil in the heavenly realms" (Eph. 6:12).

Here are some further thoughts as you approach this situation:

A. *Be sure you've got the facts.* Don't go into this battle unarmed. Know what truths you want to present to your teen from the Scriptures, and know what kind of music they are actually listening to. Don't say, "I don't like it" or "I don't think it's good for you." Any teen can deal with this kind of objection with a simple dodge: "But it's just entertainment, and it's not affecting me." Hopefully, what we've shown you in this book will give you the helpful tools you need to convince your teen that what he listens to with his ears can influence his heart and his relationship with the Lord, if he has one. If he doesn't know the Lord, this approach may open the door to show him or her the need to have a close relationship with God.

Amy Stephens says, "Pray hard and pick your battles! There should be negotiable boundaries and non-negotiable rules. Keep in mind that most children simply follow the crowd, but you will want your son or daughter to exhibit leadership in the face of opposition. That leadership involves not accepting destructive messages that are sprinkled in seemingly good entertainment."

B. *Discuss with your teen what you have seen and heard and what you are thinking.* Hear them out. But then be unwavering when it comes to music that exalts drugs, illicit sex, drunkenness, and satanic rituals. If the kids are younger, perhaps you will need to take a firmer hand and confiscate their music albums. But if you do this, don't destroy the albums. Tell the child that you will store them away and return them when he or she is old enough to make his or her own decision.

C. *Don't make God the fall guy.* If it comes down to having to actually destroy an album or of cleansing your house of certain music CDs or tapes, don't push the blame off on God: "God told me to do this." Such tactics will only harden your child's heart and breed resentment toward God. This doesn't mean you shouldn't present scriptural truth to back up why you think a course of action is necessary. Simply quoting a few key verses can stimulate thinking about these things. Some powerful verses to use are as follows:

> Do not get drunk on wine, which leads to debauchery. Instead, be filled with the Spirit. (Eph. 5:18)
> But you, man of God, flee from all this, and pursue righteousness, godliness, faith, love, endurance and gentleness. (1 Tim. 6:11)
> Flee from sexual immorality. (1 Cor. 6:18)
> But seek first his kingdom and his righteousness, and all these things will be given to you as well. (Matt. 6:33)

> Finally, brothers, whatever is true, whatever is noble, whatever is right, whatever is pure, whatever is lovely, whatever is admirable—if anything is excellent or praiseworthy—think about such things. (Phil. 4:8)
>
> But among you there must not be even a hint of sexual immorality, or of any kind of impurity, or of greed, because these are improper for God's holy people. Nor should there be obscenity, foolish talk or coarse joking, which are out of place. . . . No immoral, impure or greedy person—such a man is an idolater—has any inheritance in the kingdom of Christ and of God. . . . Therefore do not be partners with them. (Eph. 5:3–7)

All these verses and many others emphasize the truth that we must not allow our minds and hearts to be subverted by outside forces that seek to control and destroy us. An honest, straightforward presentation of these truths, backed by a life that observes them on a daily basis, goes a long way. The Spirit of God can speak to a hard heart or closed mind that all your own arguments may not penetrate.

D. *Be discerning.* Remember that we have said not all rock music is perverse or evil. There are many neutral and even socially redeeming bands out there who have messages that need to be heard. Many performers want to write good, solid love songs, or songs for clean entertainment or fun. They enjoy telling a story and setting it to lively music.

So don't annihilate all your teens' preferences in rock music. Rather, work and pray to help them become discerning people that are able to make the kinds of choices that come with adulthood. This is far more important than forcing them to reject certain performers without their having a good understanding of why they are asked to do so.

E. *Replace the old with the new.* Offer to replace bad albums with good ones at your expense. Take them to a Christian bookstore. Let them browse through the music and listen to the demos in the listening stations provided in most stores. Take them to Christian rock concerts. Immerse them in good rock music and they won't have time for the bad.

In the end, the purpose of this is to help teens make wiser entertainment choices. Once they've seen the evil of some of the music they may listen to, be prepared to fill the vacuum with some realistic alternatives (see chapter 8). But be prepared for a battle. Individual music tastes are powerful and very personal. What appeals to you or even other Christian teens may not appeal to your teen. Be prepared to continue this battle on a weekly, if not daily, basis. No teen who has devoted himself or herself to a performer or genre of music will find these choices easy.

Ultimately, your desire should be to present your family before God, a holy vessel for His Spirit. He never said it would be easy, but He does assure us it will be worth the journey. "Come to me, all you who are weary and burdened, and I will give you rest. Take my yoke upon you and learn from me, for I am gentle and humble in heart, and you will find rest for your souls. For my yoke is easy and my burden is light" (Matt. 11:28–30).

CHAPTER ELEVEN

Rock Music Questions and Answers

Any teen or parent who reads this book will probably raise questions we haven't answered. In our Truth About Rock seminars, we've engaged in some mortal and moral combats that would rival any rock concert for excitement. We know there are legitimate questions everyone has when they confront something as controversial as this book. So we're willing and open to what you have to ask. In fact, that's why we've included this section, to try to pull together any loose ends we've left in the process of trying to convince you to rethink your priorities and commitments about rock music.

People raise questions for many reasons. Some are honestly tussling with an issue, and they desire an honest answer. We're always ready to supply one in such cases.

Other people raise questions figuring we don't have any answers. They hope to nail us with something so tough and true our whole house will come tumbling down. To those we say, all we can do is try. Give us a chance, and I think you'll be pleased and surprised.

Finally, there are the folks who think they see a hole in our logic, and they wish to exploit it, relieving themselves of the responsibility of dealing with the plain facts. It's those people to whom we most appeal: Reject the facts at your own peril. All of us will answer for our lives to Jesus. We tremble to think that some of us will have to explain hours and hours of listening pleasure that will be burned up and reduced to ashes. Our hope is that all of our lives will count for Him who gave His all for us. So we plead with you, don't dodge the issues. Face them squarely, prayerfully, honestly. We're confident you'll never regret it.

Why haven't you said anything about my favorite rock group?

The rock scene is dynamic, always in a state of flux. Today's heroes may be tomorrow's saps. Tomorrow's stars may stay a year or two and then disappear like so many "one-hit wonders."

But it doesn't matter. Jesus told us we will recognize false leaders and teachers "by their fruit" (Matt. 7:16). A rock group with a hidden agenda, an immoral lifestyle, hideous lyrics, gross graphics, and hedonistic goals will soon show themselves for who they are. All you have to do is a little research to find out what your favorite performers stand for and live for.

Remember, we're not trying to tell you who you should listen to and who you should not listen to. Our purpose is to give you scriptural and reasonable guidelines that can help you to make your own musical and entertainment choices. We want you to "own" your beliefs and decisions, not be persuaded against your will. We will all answer to God for our own choices. We have given you some tools. If you *want* to know the truth, you will find it.

Will listening to secular rock music send me to hell?

Neither music nor movies nor TV nor anything else you do or enjoy can send you to hell. Only one person can consign you to damnation, and that is yourself. The apostle Paul told the Corinthians, "For we must all appear before the judgment seat of Christ, that each one may receive what is due him for the things done while in the body, whether good or bad" (2 Cor. 5:10). Those are words of great encouragement and hope and also of great pain and fear. One day each of us will answer to Jesus for everything we've done—thought, word, and deed.

The danger in rock music is that its influence can cause us to forsake the truth and indulge in a lifestyle that ultimately leads to hell. If we reject Christ because we revere a rock star's stand on religion, or we espouse Christ but live a life that counts for nothing in His kingdom, we are the losers. Rock stars will stand before God, too. They'll answer for the things they've done and for the people they've led astray.

Is there anything wrong with the music in rock—that is, the sound, the beat, the drums, the guitar riffs...?

Music is a gift of God. The eight-note "scale" or octave was imbedded into the heart of the universe by the Lord, not by the devil. Though some have tried to say that the rhythm or beat in rock music is like music used by witch doctors in Africa to excite demons and incite people, it's a myth and a racist one at that. No beat or syncopation is intrinsically evil. It's like saying strawberries or corn is evil. Beat and rhythm are part of the universe in which we live. God put it there.

Rock music becomes evil when rock stars take the beat, the music, the rhythm, and put words to it that incite a crowd to sin— profanity, violence, use of drugs or alcohol, sexual immorality, or other illicit practices. People can certainly be moved by music. However, more often than not, it is what the music represents that has the greater effect. We mentioned before Elton John's "Candle in the Wind," played and sung at Princess Diana's funeral. This was moving for the circumstances, the words, and the manner in which it was presented. Marilyn Manson, on the other hand, incites a crowd with profanity, immoral displays on stage, and mini-sermons against Christianity. It is how Manson uses music to influence people to commit sinful acts that makes it evil. Music is neutral but can be "used" for good or evil. A knife is neutral, but it can be used to prepare food to sustain life, or it can be used to end a life.

Haven't studies shown that TV violence and sex has no real influence on its viewers? Isn't it the same with rock music? Why do you think a rock star can influence me to sin? I just like the songs.

Anyone who believes such studies should ask himself, Why does TV make so much money from advertising? Advertisers certainly don't buy into the belief that TV can't influence people to do anything. During the Super Bowl, advertisers spend $1.5 million on a thirty-second spot believing they can influence behavior. Kids listen to thousands of hours of rock music and assume they are not affected.

Everyone we come into contact with influences us in some way—teachers, preachers, parents, siblings, friends, co-workers—everyone who touches our life has an effect on us. We can react with anger, love, fear, or adoration. But there is a reaction, even if it's indifference.

To say that rock stars don't have an influence on anyone is pure foolishness. In reality, rock stars often determine what clothes we wear, how we wear our hair, what restaurants and shows we go to, what movies we see, what people we quote, what TV shows we watch, and so on. Every teen in high school can identify members of a group by what they wear, how they talk, and what they do: jocks, nerds, preppies, and punks have all been influenced by someone. In many cases, it's what rock stars are promoting, saying, or "preaching." The Beatles made the mop-top haircut, marijuana, and TM fashionable simply by promoting their own lifestyle. Today nose, mouth, and eyebrow rings, demonic symbols such as the pentagram, and punk haircuts, mosh pits, and the like have become popular because rock stars have sported them.

You might argue that this is all hype, that rock stars do obnoxious and immoral things as a "joke"; to make news, to have fun.

Undoubtedly, in some cases this may be true. These people have become jaded and callused by their past deeds and now perform gross acts as part of their "show." But Scripture doesn't mince words: "Bad company corrupts good morals" (1 Cor. 15:33, NASB).

Isn't what you're talking about censorship? Doesn't our Bill of Rights guarantee freedom of speech? You are trying to censor everyone you don't like.

Years ago manufacturers could employ children, work them fourteen to sixteen hours a day, and then pay them a pittance for their labors. Laws "censored" this evil.

Not so many years ago, African-Americans couldn't use certain rest rooms, go into certain buildings, or sit at the front of buses because they were black. New laws "censored" this evil.

There was a time when a person could be denied work because of their gender, race, creed, or religion. This is no longer true because laws "censored" that "right" on the part of employers.

We're not saying rock music should be censored and rock musicians' right to express themselves suppressed. We're only asking that the laws already on the books be enforced. For instance, there's U.S. Code Title 18, Section 1464, which says, "Whoever utters any obscene, indecent, or profane language by means of radio communications shall be fined not more than $10,000 or imprisoned not more than two years or both." This law clearly prohibits the airplay of obscene rock lyrics. However, it is rarely enforced.

In the movie world, there is a rating system designed to help parents determine when and if their children should see certain movies. This system has its problems, and we're not saying it's perfect. However, it does help parents make decisions about movies for their children.

There is a Parental Advisory sticker placed on some albums. However, it is not a consistent system (much like the movie ratings). Parents should make themselves aware of the ratings when selecting music for their children or for their teens to listen to. This is not censorship; it is good parenting. Every parent has a responsibility before God to raise their children in the faith and to train them in moral, ethical, and biblical standards. To shirk this duty invites the worst sort of censure from the Bible. Every parent should have the right to help their children make good and sensible moral choices in all areas, including rock music. A system like this is not going to be perfect, but it could help stop the rising tide of filth being produced by many rock groups today.

Why is rock music so popular with teens?

I've pondered this question for years, wondering just what attracts teens to this type of music so readily. The easy answer is that their friends like it, so it must be good. Peer influence generally is the strongest form of influence among teens.

Upon deeper examination, I feel rock music is popular because it is so easy and inviting. A parent, teacher, or youth pastor demands a certain standard of performance, achievement, or respect from the young person. But the rock musician screams, "Don't worry about all that . . . we accept you just the way you are. We have no standards, no goals . . . Come on—join the party!"

Teens want to be accepted, and they find willing reception in the rock music industry.

If you guys are supposed to be such great resources, why do you quote so few lines from each song? Shouldn't you quote the whole song to put it in context or are you trying to hide the "good" lyrics?

It is against the copyright laws of the United States to reprint an entire song without first securing permission and paying an appropriate royalty fee. In fact, two record companies began lawsuits against us years ago, claiming we couldn't even quote "two words from any of [their] songs."

We hired a copyright attorney who researched the matter and found that under the Fair Use Clause in the Copyright Statute that we could quote small portions of any song we chose to critique. He wrote those two record companies citing the appropriate statute, and they dropped their efforts to sue us.

You keep saying lyrics are a big part of the problem. But I don't really listen to lyrics, just the tune. The words don't matter. How is this going to affect me?

Seventy percent of people who buy rock albums buy them because of the beat, the tune, or the group performing it. They rarely buy an album for the lyrics. However, when we play snatches of tunes in our Truth About Rock seminars and stop them in the middle, the kids finish singing the song. They don't even realize how well they know the lyrics.

Music is a spiritual medium. It goes beyond the mind and touches the heart and the soul. It reaches us in the deepest part of our beings. That's why its influence is so powerful and why people pay billions of dollars a year to support the industry. Music can give us rest and quiet, peace in our inner beings. We can listen to a tune and because of the words feel calm, happy, inspired, or uplifted. We can also be moved to actions we'd never dream of doing on our own. Look at the kids in the mosh pit. Does that make any sense? Look at the oddest, most ridiculous hair styles imaginable. Why are they wearing their hair that way? How can they think it is attractive? Their favorite performers are wearing their hair that way. Therefore, it *must* be cool.

When you can play a song on the radio and have kids as young as six singing along, you have a song with lyrics that have made an impact. Sure, a lot of rock music is about love, peace, happiness, breaking up and making up. But there's plenty of the opposite, too. And that's the danger. When you think your heart is being filled with love, peace, and joy, the performer slips in the one ounce of poison that can kill you.

As we have said many times in this book, teens listen to rock music on an average of six hours a day, often playing a single song over and over for hours. If the lyrics on that song are suggesting that they engage in evil acts—drugs, violence, suicide—is it possible that listeners are deriving some pleasure in imagining themselves doing those things?

Someone once said, "Sow a thought, reap a deed. Sow a deed, reap a habit. Sow a habit, reap a lifestyle. Sow a lifestyle, reap a destiny." Lyrics are thoughts put into words that sink into the minds and hearts of listeners. In some it may only provoke a reaction of pleasure. But in others it could lead to wrongdoing. Herein lies the danger. Sooner or later everyone who listens to a significant amount of rock music will be influenced.

Why are you picking on rock music? Don't country, easy listening, blues, jazz, and other styles have many of the same problems?

If anything, our heart is with young people, teens who are on the cusp of life and the cutting edge of adulthood. What influences they take with them into adulthood will affect their children and the generations to come. We find that while all those other styles of music have their own problems, rock still has the biggest influence, especially on young people. Go to any music store and check out what's on the shelves. There is more rock than anything else. Observe who visits most of the aisles and displays of rock music: teens.

Actually, we are not "picking" on anything. It just so happens that our expertise is with rock, and that's what we write about. Only a few others have ever written enough about rock music to expose the things in it that are contrary to truth and light. This is our niche, our bailiwick, so to speak. We feel called by God to this work.

Why do you cite such groups as the Beatles and Doors who aren't even together anymore?

Amazingly enough, those two groups, among others, have experienced resurgences in recent years. Oliver Stone did a movie (*The Doors*) on the life of Jim Morrison, lead singer of the Doors, and their music as a result received a lot of airplay. The Beatles also recently released their two anthologies, which were two of the best-selling CDs at the time. Their music continues to have an impact.

In addition, many other groups who were around in the '60s, '70s, and '80s are still together or have rejoined to do new gigs. REO Speedwagon, KISS, Journey, Foreigner, Styx, AC/DC, and many others are cutting records and cruising the concert circuits with their music. The Rolling Stones signed a multimillion-dollar contract for their "Bridge to Babylon" tour.

The main consideration is that all these groups feed off one another. The Beatles were influenced by Elvis, who affected nearly everyone. It was the lascivious performances of "Elvis the pelvis" in the '50s that paved the way for the lusty Ozzy Osbourne and David Bowie. Their antics spawned more outrageous material from Guns N' Roses and Marilyn Manson.

Rock stars' songs and lyrics survive, too, on oldies stations that fill the airwaves in every U.S. city. Their influence and antics are still covered by *Entertainment Weekly, People*, and the plethora of teen magazines covering the rock scene.

Rock music isn't static. Their wild and disgusting stage acts continue to draw fans and have an effect on today's and tomorrow's society.

Rock music is an art, just like the art of Van Gogh and Rembrandt, Beethoven and Bach. Why do you want to take away rock musicians' freedom to express themselves?

What passes for art in our culture is up for grabs. Everything from the monastic chants of the Middle Ages to the Alanis Morissette's of the present is called art. We're not here to redefine art or even censor rock musicians' right to express themselves. We just wish they could "express themselves" in places and to people and in ways that don't cause moral and spiritual harm. Giving rock musicians a carte blanche right to spew over the airwaves any filth that has coursed their brains is not only foolish, it is reckless.

As we have debated hundreds of disc jockeys on air, many of them privately have admitted to us that they *do not allow their own children to listen to their radio station!* The height of hypocrisy.

Young people *are* being affected. Lives are being changed—usually for the worse. Rebellion is urged and applauded. Hatred, misogyny, hedonism, and immorality are all espoused as the "way, truth, and life" of an almost cultic religion. Though it may not have an immediate effect on you or people you know, it does have an effect. Consider that only one in ten people who ever take a drink become alcoholics. But what if you are the one in ten?

Our concern is that these so-called rock stars are viewed as models and leaders to be followed. Kurt Cobain was once touted as rock's newest and greatest "messiah." People lauded him as an archetype of the future, someone who had a real grip on what was tearing out the hearts of young people. He ended up in his last days a hopeless heroin addict and a desperate threat to his wife and child. It's tragic that his inner tormentors led him to suicide, but he is ultimately responsible for his own fall. And if others imitate him, might they not soon find themselves with a blown mind longing only for death? Still, this man is emulated and revered, often by people who don't know what his life was like. Our purpose here is to expose the truth. What you do with it is your privilege and responsibility.

Aren't you trying to shield young people from real life? How will they cope with the real world if they don't know what it's like?

Would you expose a child to the HIV virus? Would you encourage a young person to drink alcohol until drunk or sniff lines of cocaine until stoned, and then lie down with bisexuals who could be carrying any number of diseases?

Of course not. And yet this is what is often espoused at the rock concerts and in the music of these so-called artists. No thinking parent puts his child into circumstances that can cause irreparable harm. In fact, the parent warns the child to stay away from such things and even shows that child how disastrous a flirtation with such practices can be. When Jesus faced Satan in the wilderness, He only did so after fasting for forty days and nights so that He had the spiritual strength and perceptiveness to win. So a parent prepares his or her children and shows them the right way, not all the possible ways that one could go.

In our age, we can be sure that any child who visits the playground or the mall will receive plenty of exposure to what the world is like. To take that a step further and encourage them to walk into the lions' den of much of modern rock music is foolhardy and irresponsible. God will ultimately call every parent into account for the media he allowed his child to listen to or observe. We cannot shrink from the task. We must take rock by the horns and expose it for what it is, leading children into the truth that will truly set them free.

Are you saying that I shouldn't listen to any secular rock music, ever?

Not at all. We readily admit that some rock is commendable. Some of its music is entertaining and fun, without the lurid lyrics, appeal to hedonism, or use of drugs or other substances. But we have to ask the question sooner or later: What *good* does listening to secular rock music do? Does it move me closer to Jesus? Does it help me in my spiritual life? Does it build family and community relationships? Does it make me think thoughts that glorify God and holiness?

Paul said, "Each of us will give an account of himself to God"

(Rom. 14:12). And, "Be very careful, then, how you live—not as unwise but as wise, making the most of every opportunity, because the days are evil" (Eph. 5:15–16). Is life simply the search for better entertainment? Are we wise to use the time and resources allotted to us in the support and encouragement of secular rock music? When we stand before Christ, will we relish answering to Him as to why we spend six hours a day listening to secular rock music?

It's your choice. Neither we nor your parents nor anyone else can force you to agree with this position. You will answer for yourself. It has been our hope in writing this, though, that you will now have the tools and power to make not only better choices but the best ones.

If I shouldn't listen to secular rock music, what should I listen to?

The real question is: What is the best way for me to use my time as a Christian and as a follower of Jesus Christ?

Paul told the Corinthians that every activity of their lives should glorify the Lord (1 Cor. 10:31); he taught the Ephesians to "make the most of every opportunity" in an evil world (Eph. 5:15); and he advised the Galatians to "live by the Spirit" (Gal. 5:16). By so doing, they would not give in to the desires of the flesh.

Years ago a book was written called *In His Steps*. It was a novel in which Christians submitted everything they did and planned to do to one question: What would Jesus do? Can you honestly answer that Jesus would spend six hours a day listening to the radio, MTV, music videos, or CDs, of any kind? Do you think He would revel in a KISS concert? Or dance to tunes by AC/DC or the Rolling Stones?

We know that Jesus would not shun the people involved in such things, but He would reach out to them and build a relationship with them in order to take them past their wrong desires and on to wholesome desires. When He talked to Zaccheus, the tax collector made an about-face and vowed to pay four times what he owed anyone. When Jesus conversed with the woman at the well, she felt such conviction for her sins that she went and evangelized a whole city. In fact, every time you see Jesus, He is reaching out to people. Just as He was accused in His day of dining with "taxgatherers and sinners," He would probably be accused of hobnobbing with "Hollywood celebrities" and rock stars today—not to promote their lifestyles, but to win their friendship and hopefully bring them to repentance and faith.

A question like "What am I supposed to listen to?" is really the wrong question. It's not what am I supposed to listen to, but why. If what you listen to ends up being cheap entertainment that is little more than a waste of time and money, then why do it? If it doesn't help you grow in your spiritual life and become more committed to the Lord, then why bother with it? If it can't strengthen you in your family and community relationships, then what's the point? It's that simple. And if you truly want an alternative, read chapter 8.

CHAPTER TWELVE

Rock Artists A to Z

There are two basic purposes for this chapter, and they need to be considered separately. *The first purpose is to give information to readers so that they can wisely choose material for their musical encouragement, exhortation, and entertainment.* More than anything else this involves four things for the reader: earnest prayer for guidance, an effort to understand biblical guidelines for the Christian life, a careful evaluation of the contents of the music of various artists, and an increased discernment of the strengths and weaknesses of one's Christian walk.

The second purpose is to assist readers in identifying the worldviews of the artists through the lyrics they sing. This stimulates meaningful discussion with families and friends; it also highlights the vast chasm separating life in Christ from service to sin and self. We hope that raising the issues this music confronts and presents will enhance communication regarding the state of our culture and how it can be reached with the love, truth, hope, and grace of Jesus Christ.

Christian missionary and visionary John Fischer says, "It's always rude to speak before you listen." He notes that as followers of Christ we rarely take the time and the trouble to walk in the world's shoes to truly understand and have compassion for those who have not been transformed.

For Christians, then, entering someone else's world means choosing to listen and learn before reacting. It's important to remember that before we knew the love of God in Christ, we were lost and in bondage to sin. We couldn't abstain from sinfulness before we received the grace of God's forgiveness.

This being true, Christians will realize that before they try to convince the world that it should obey the teachings of Christ, they need to stress the miracle of salvation and the gift of Christ's sacrifice. In short, it's futile to expect someone to obey the lordship of Jesus Christ before they see the truth of Jesus Christ as Savior.

It's also true that *every* talent is a gift from God. These abilities are a loan from Him and can be used by Him regardless of a person's decisions for or against Him. Even music artists who wouldn't appreciate being tagged as "in God's service" can fulfill His purposes. Like Caiaphas, they can speak His truths (John 11:49–52). Therefore, their music can bring about at least two results. First, some "secular" material will glorify God by lifting up things in harmony with His character. Second, the aspects of their material that are contrary to God give us important clues about the reasons our culture stumbles before reaching Christ in its search for truth and significance.

Effectively evaluating, confronting, and confirming the music of non-Christians only happens through God's love, mercy, and Spirit. We need to talk *with* our culture rather than *at* it. Non-believers can certainly see through our façades if we don't care enough to listen to them. Remember that Jesus responded to the most damnable acts in history by pleading, "Father, forgive them, for they don't know what they're doing."

(Readers should be aware that song lyrics were, for the most part, the primary source for comments in this evaluative section. Unless otherwise noted, lifestyles, concerts, graphics/art, etc. were considered in earlier sections of this book. Also, the criteria for inclusion in this section were album sales and levels of popularity according to established standards such as Billboard's Top 200.)

Aaliyah

Aaliyah's lyrical focus is romantic love. A great percentage of it exalts themes glorifying to God: passion, commitment, dedication, self-sacrifice, patience, vulnerability, and truthfulness. There are times, however, when it would be legitimate to question the nature of the relationship of the man and the woman in the songs. Lyrics include coarse references.

Ace of Base

Ace of Base can be easily tagged "feel good" music, for many topics and sentiments are fairly basic thoughts about relationships. Much of the band's content, though, burrows more deeply into the soul, vulnerably sharing honest thoughts and feelings about joy, sadness, peace, frustration, and love. Ace of Base triumphs faithfulness, unity, self-sacrifice, and above all, hope, singing even in the midst of great fear and loneliness, "Why do you ask why I'm not blaming my god? I'll tell you what—He was the only one there." While some songs contain lyrics listeners will want to examine individually, Ace of Base generally focuses upon what is pure and excellent.

Aerosmith

Aerosmith, more than anything else, is about entertaining and giving in to lust and debauchery. Steven Tyler advocates that people have as much sex as possible, and his music seconds this idea without conditions given, graphically illustrating sexual immorality in myriad ways. Some songs include spiritual reflection and at times comment on the issues of evil in its different forms, but the searching ends there: Aerosmith rejects Jesus Christ in favor of music and sex. Early on, the band was notorious for the overindulgences with drugs and alcohol that temporarily broke them up. In this area they have completely altered their course and are substance-free. Sadly, they stopped short of finding the true source of life and hope. Lyrics contain frequent and explicit sexual imagery along with obscenities and endorsements of violence.

Alice In Chains

Alice In Chains vacillates between hatred and apathy, rage and despair in the course of dealing with ravaging depression and devastating drug addiction. Lyrics suggest that the self is despised and that there is no hope for the soul perceived as sick and filthy. Alice In Chains often includes distorted biblical and anti-biblical allusions, such as "Jesus Christ—deny your maker." Lyrics also contain obscenities and graphic references.

Tori Amos

The music of Tori Amos is about a woman who has endured much pain and loneliness (including a devastating rape when she was twenty-two) and who wants to be accepted and embraced for who she is. Her vulnerable and straightforward messages show that she values faithfulness, genuine love, and self-discovery. Amos writes of her ongoing disillusionment with God; many of her lyrics contain mixed inferences to both spirituality and sexuality. She explains this by stating her belief that separating these two entities is contrary to reconciling a person to herself and her natures. In a *Hot Press* interview with Joe Jackson, Amos states that "I've always believed that Jesus Christ really liked Mary Magdalene and that if He was, as He claimed to be, a whole man, He had to have sexual relations with her. So, in my deepest private moments, I've wanted Christ to be the boyfriend I've been waiting for. And a lot of Christian girls have a crush on Jesus. I may have felt guilty at the thought of wanting to do it with Jesus, but then I say, 'Why not? He *was* a man.' " [Comment: But He was also God. In the Incarnation, Jesus did not *subtract* Godhood; instead, He *added* manhood.] She mocks the suffering Savior portrait of Jesus (and other types) offered by the church and her father as a minister. Lyrics contain profanity and various types of graphic references.

Fiona Apple

Apple believes that life equals experience; therefore, in order to be artistically truthful, life must be shared and communicated honestly, whether its yields are regarded as good or bad, positive or negative. Her music is reflective of her forthrightness. Most prominently, her heart is devastated and hollow from broken relationships. In such cases, she says that even when she has known she would be mortally wounded by being toyed with and used, she has proceeded into relationships anyway because the short-term benefits were too good to pass up. Confusion and emptiness have been the results, and she pensively laments that "the child is gone"; there is no more innocence to be known through the pain. She is contrite for having hurt a former friend, advocating truthfulness and vulnerability for future relationships. Unfortunately, her videos are sensual and sexual in their portrayal of her music.

Aqua

Aqua's hit single "Barbie Girl" brought hefty lawsuits from Mattel for what the toy manufacturer termed trademark infringement and the association of sexual and other unsavory themes with the Barbie™ doll. Among the song's lyrics are "Brush my hair, undress me everywhere," "I'm a bimbo blonde girl," and "Kiss me here, touch me there, hanky-panky." The Scandinavian foursome responded that the song is not a parody but rather is social commentary. In a Canadian Music Television interview the band claims that Aqua really has no message except, "Be happy. It's not that deep, it's just . . . pop music." Aqua issues a powerful challenge for men: Turn and face the devastation you create when you choose to leave and reject those who love you. Some lyrics contain sexual references.

Arrested Development

Arrested Development calls for a spiritual revolution, rejecting immoral responses to social woes and challenging all humankind to embrace self-discipline. A primary focus of the band is to change our political and cultural ways of thinking: "Give a man a fish, and he'll eat for a day; teach him how to fish, and he'll eat forever." Honor is lavished upon single parents who choose to give the gift of life to their children, and fathers are dared to take responsibility for the families they help to create. Lyrics also offer a memorable tribute to a homeless man, delighting in his love and wisdom and pointing out that while we are prone to overlook and even judge such a person, he has spiritual wealth that most of us cannot fathom. Arrested Development warns us that unforgiveness and resentment only bring enslavement and death as they sadly narrate disrespect and subsequent violence between brothers. They also accuse Satan of deception, asserting that we have listened to his encouragement to serve ourselves and thus have denied our Creator. Arrested Development's suggestions for being freed and unblinded: Seek the truth, thank the Lord of life, and ask for wisdom and discernment.

Susan Ashton

Ashton in every way directs her listeners' attention to Christ, asserting that rather than trusting in man, they should place faith in the unchanging God. She warns of not being on guard against the temptation that leads to prideful sin and hardness of heart. Lyrics admonish us to move through our difficulties with the help of Christ, who will bring forgiveness, healing, and growth. Amid confusion and fear, Ashton rejoices in hope and freedom. She also encourages sacrificial and faithful love so that we model the way Jesus loves us.

Audio Adrenaline

Audio Adrenaline displays thankfulness for the saving grace of Jesus, exalting and worshiping Him in service and adoration. They emphasize that everything we are and have is a gift from Christ; therefore, we are to place our faith in and be obedient to Him. Audio Adrenaline tells of their struggles with human nature and difficult emotions, offering the solutions of prayer and evangelism.

Babyface

Babyface presents truly beautiful pictures of relational love and friendship, advocating faithfulness, commitment, vulnerability, and sacrifice. He captures a sense of thankfulness for love that glorifies passion and honors marriage and family. [Comment: A caution should be heeded: This love shouldn't be intended to replace God but to focus upon Him as its foundation. Human "love" without God tries to fill in too much of the picture, attempting to satisfy a desire it is incapable of satiating.] Some songs contain graphic sexual expressions.

Bad Religion

Bad Religion (Greg Graffin) sees the world as sinful and decayed, full of horror and chaos. Graffin embraces the theories of science but rejects God as revealed in Jesus Christ. He sees a world that was hopeless from the start and will come to its end in the same way: "F—— Armageddon, this is hell." Bad Religion isn't necessarily humanistic, either: Man is helplessly out of control and worthless.

In short, every cause is "empty"—even his own. Anger, depression, fear, confusion, and hatred are more than understandable coming from this worldview. Bad Religion says, "It's all right to have faith in god," but what "god" is unclear.

Graffin holds special contempt for Jews and Christians and their respective faiths. He slashes them for being so blind as to allegedly trust in God and then to blame Him for all of their (and the world's) troubles. Bad Religion attacks God for what they perceive as His responsibility for evil. Note these lyrics: "I don't know what stopped Jesus Christ from turning every stone into bread. And I don't remember hearing how Moses reacted when the innocent firstborn sons lay dead. Well, I guess God was a lot more demonstrative back when He flamboyantly parted the sea. Now everybody's praying. Don't prey on me." Ultimately, to Bad Religion, faith is meaningless: "I heard them say that the meek shall reign on earth; phantasmal myriads of sane bucolic birth. I've seen the rapture in a starving baby's eyes; Inchoate beatitude, the Lord of the Flies. . . . Brother, you'd better get down on your knees and pray; 1,000 more fools are being born every f——ing day. And they try to tell me that the lamb is on the way." Thus, only death is to be desired: "Look at all the living and you'll ask yourself why—Oh why do we pity the dead?"

Lyrics contain violence, obscenities, and sexual imagery.

Erykah Badu

Badu's messages are politically conscious and emotionally charged. Her blend of spiritualism is mixed and cryptic—she frequently invokes both God and wisdom. She also suggests ties to certain New Age tendencies. Perhaps she describes it best herself in titling her recent album "Baduizm." Some lyrics contain obscenities and sexual expressions.

Ant Banks

Ant Banks' music is violence, alcohol, and drug abuse, profanity, vile innuendo, and sexual atrocities against women.

The Beastie Boys

The recurrent themes coming from the mikes of the Beastie Boys are indignant rebellion, frequent profanity, and general crudeness. Buddhist leanings and sentiments surface at times, but for the most part the Beastie Boys produce raging, angry noise.

Beck

Beck's expressions are full of attempts to convince listeners to realize what losers we all are (occasionally crudely). His primary aim seems to be to expose the ultimate pointlessness and absurdity of our existence. He does not elaborate on what he thinks should change; there is some question as to whether Beck is reflecting himself in his music or merely echoing the current themes of the culture.

Better Than Ezra

Better Than Ezra portrays a sad but resilient young soul seen as misunderstood by the world and wounded by his parents. Confused and somewhat jaded, he is encouraged not to listen to what others say—they're not going to take care of him and they don't have his best interests in mind, so he is to be exactly who he is and look out for number one. Lyrics promote self-preservation but don't warn about guarding against selfishness and apathy. Better Than Ezra provides glimpses of depression and possible mental illness; lyrics praise faithful friendship and warn against jealousy. Some songs contain sexual imagery.

Big Head Todd and the Monsters

Big Head Todd demonstrates a painful awareness of the soul's emptiness while searching for genuine love and significance in life.

While lyrics extol the value of unconditional commitment and faithfulness in relationships, the band doesn't find a true answer for its loneliness. Instead, Big Head Todd concludes that alcohol brings peace amid futility and that ultimately, rather than having a purpose, life is a meaningless, cyclical pattern of people and events.

The Black Crowes

The music of the Black Crowes reflects weariness with life's never-ending struggles and a conclusion that alcohol and drugs alone can be trusted to bring deliverance. Lyrics ridicule faith in any other source, suggesting that everything else will eventually fail, including the Lord: "Jesus can't save you, though it's nice to think he'd try. . . ." Songs about relationships generally focus upon pain leading to indifference and bitterness leading to unforgiveness. While certain lyrics are both vulnerably honest and touchingly pure, many are about using women to meet men's needs rather than about love. The Black Crowes use both implicit and explicit graphic sexual references and profanity.

BLACKstreet

BLACKstreet's music is encompassed by romantic love. Some songs beg a lover not to leave; often, lyrics affirm such praiseworthy themes as faithfulness and endurance. Lyrics contain profanity and sexual innuendo that invites illicit activity; one song focuses upon the singer's obsession with a prostitute.

Mary J. Blige

Blige sings primarily of love, whether love lost, love present, or love desired. Many lyrics triumph commitment, honesty, and faithfulness, but Blige often places love and sexual activity in the wrong order, being physically involved with men she has known as friends or acquaintances. Some of her material contains profanity and crude references.

Blind Melon

Blind Melon's Shannon Hoon believed that blindness is preferable to truth because he felt that truth doesn't heal the deepest wounds of the soul. While at times demonstrating a clear knowledge of personal sinfulness and the truth that haunted his being, Hoon cursed Christianity and those who pursued the salvation of his soul. He was desperately lonely and longed to find significance and meaning for his life, yet he saw his hope repeatedly extinguished, and he subsequently resigned his tormented mind to the belief that only drugs (temporarily) and death (ultimately) would release him from his anguish.

Hoon was consistently dismayed and angry at being scrutinized and criticized, responding with counter-rejection of others and a stated desire to have only freedom and peace. He found temporary respite in the knowledge that he was to become a father, earnestly pleading for revitalization and renewal and seeking help in overcoming his crippling drug addictions.

But all philosophy, outside of God's truth, falls short. Hoon tragically relapsed and ended his life with a drug overdose, dramatizing that his answers did not work.

Blues Traveler

Blues Traveler should be commended for its lyrical commitment to taking responsibility for one's life and recognizing that choices have definite consequences. Also, the band encourages listeners to discover what is truly inside of them and to confront it honestly. However, the conclusions that Blues Traveler draws for its own problems are selfish, thoughtless, and narcissistic. Some lyrics contain profanity and lewd sexual references.

Blur

Blur's earlier recordings are a plea for hope, while the latest album ("Blur") seems to represent a determination that there isn't any. "The Great Escape" saw life through a visor of endless depression that perceived existence as fading into stereotypical blandness and irrelevance. Brief insights into dreams of love and joy are shattered by the blur life becomes as its brutal realities take their toll on our lives. Blur is a picture of life without a future and a desire to find if there is anything more. Blur seems to suggest that those people who "appear" to be "best" are actually likely to be covering the truth and perhaps more deranged than anyone else. Lyrics contain "adult" themes and references.

Bone Thugs-N-Harmony

Bone Thugs-N-Harmony's gruesome material consists of profanity, violence, background sexual activity sound effects, gang-related posturing and threats, alcohol and drug abuse, cop killing, crime, occult references (Ouija board), and sexual assault against women.

Boyz II Men

Much of the Boyz' music is a tribute to a host of solid ideals, including fidelity and commitment in relationships, nostalgic remembrance of loved ones and good times gone by, and perseverance through periods of depression or transition. Some songs are questionable, and "I'll Make Love to You," a song about passionate physical love between a man and woman, might be too "adult" for young people.

Brandy

Brandy affirms the valuable principle of staying true to friendship even in the hardest of times. Her music also embraces the endurance of seasons of pain in healthy ways, determining to learn from struggle and remembering that life will go on even while grieving and sadness remain. In some ways, however, she is a notable example of how much is routinely given today's generation to bear. [Comment: In relation to this, Brandy was singing about sexual passion before she was of legal driving age; one wonders whether young teenagers need encouragement to develop stronger feelings for members of the opposite sex at that stage.]

Toni Braxton

Braxton's penchant for overflowing with euphoria for love at present and with wretched sadness over love gone by is deeply moving and unfailingly reflective. That this love is brought to the forefront by the mass of her music is wonderful in and of itself; however,

Braxton, like so many artists, seems to confuse love with sex, and she uses incompatible spiritual imagery to describe sexual love. (According to *Entertainment Weekly*, she once described her song "Speaking in Tongues" as the sounds people make as they make love.) While rightfully celebrating the beautiful love that can develop between two souls, Braxton focuses upon one-night stands and ill-advised exchanges of passion instead of endorsing moral integrity.

Garth Brooks

Garth Brooks's music is filled with inspiration, especially to embrace at the present moment exactly what one's heart desires. This includes not wasting any chances to make an impact or a needed change. Brooks clearly believes in God's providence, goodness, and faithfulness, and he encourages sacrifice, resilience, responsibility, friendship, passion, confidence, loyalty, and vulnerability. Brooks presents truly memorable exaltations of love and family, and in tales of heartache and regret he warns against selfishness and pride, honestly displaying struggles with lust and dishonesty. Brooks also promotes the unconditional acceptance of others.

What is so puzzling is Brooks's lyrical acceptance of violence, alcohol abuse, immoral sexual behavior, and even perhaps suicide. While he has waged and won several personal battles and is now faithfully dedicated to his family, he seems to make a distinction between the way he lives and what he chooses to sing about. Some songs contain profanity and sexual imagery.

Meredith Brooks

Brooks maintains a balance by both acknowledging life's difficulties and distancing herself from the pain of others and the world in general. On "B——h," she reveals that she sees herself as both high maintenance and enigmatic (or puzzling, or confusing). Brooks at times seems to regret the way she becomes numb or indifferent to others when she withdraws; she is also honest about her struggles with lust and deception. "I Need" gives a long list of what Brooks sees as being necessary for her well-being. Many material and intangible items are mentioned, including "a dose of the Bible" and for "my father to love me." Some lyrics contain profanity and sexual expressions.

Brotha Lynch Hung

Brotha Lynch Hung, a professing atheist and—cannibal?—includes and endorses threats of violence, references to vile sexual misuses, triumphant boasts of murder, use of marijuana, and profanity.

Bush

The name "Bush" has, admittedly, a double meaning: it is both a reference to genital anatomy and a British word for marijuana. Bush's lyrics are offerings to nihilism and misery with emotional and sexual undertones that are difficult to interpret. While this foursome may seem to be endorsing fatalism and irresponsibility, they are also begging for a solution to their misery: "Hell is where the heart is." Bush has a fixation with death and violence.

Busta Rhymes

Rhymes' profane and graphically perverse material promotes alcohol and drug abuse, the degradation and mistreatment of women, and violence and murder under the guise of gang threats that allegedly carry "the power of God."

The Butthole Surfers

The Butthole Surfers exhibit an absurd and dreary view of life filled with parody and sarcasm that reaches toward humor until one considers the tragedy of the chaos and lostness of their perspective. Most of their music is devoid of searching and speculation; the band approaches spiritual issues with songs like "The Lord Is a Monkey." Lyrics contain obscenities and vile, vivid language regarding human anatomy.

Cake

Cake has aimed to step out from an "alternative" musical genre that commonly evokes sorrows and misery in listeners. However,

Cake's outlook is also quite bleak. Many songs tell stories of loneliness and loss, and Cake paints so many pictures of one human hurting another that one gets the impression that the soul portrayed in Cake's lyrics has never seen true love in action. Cake seems discontent, bitter, and sad; at the same time they appear to be trying to maintain a focus on love and hope. Cake speaks of knowing the truth but not yet choosing to embrace it: "I hope I've got a little more time. . . . Now, Jesus wrote a blank check. Ah, one I haven't cashed yet. Still I build my towers high. . . . Still I wallow in the mire. Still I burn this earthen fire." Lyrics contain profanities, graphic portrayals of human anatomy, sexual imagery, and a mention of satanic ritual.

Cannibal Corpse

Cannibal Corpse's song titles include "Necropedophile," "Post Mortal Ejaculation," and "Addicted to Vaginal Skin." Honestly, that's just a sample; lyrics are beyond imagination.

Mariah Carey

Carey's music is full of affirmation for some of the true accompaniments of love: joy, longing, euphoria, and pain. She warns of growing up too quickly and splendidly illustrates the truth that genuinely loving others will bring us to set them free rather than to possess and stifle them. If listeners regard her lyrics in light of lifelong commitment between spouses, the message will often be inspiring. One might consider whether Carey's efforts are sufficiently broad, for at times it seems that all of life is seen to revolve around sexual expression and romantic love (even healthy things can bring disease if ingested in excess). Nevertheless, her messages are primarily positive.

Bob Carlisle

Carlisle, formerly of Allies, is famous for "Butterfly Kisses," his beautiful nostalgic tribute to his daughter. Carlisle shares his thankfulness for God's grace and mercy, praying for spiritual strengthening and renewal and lifting up his eternal hope in Christ. Lyrics glorify integrity, faith, surrender, love, service, and prayer. Carlisle also sings the praises of marital bliss as he highlights hard work, sacrifice, and honesty.

Steven Curtis Chapman

Chapman exalts Jesus Christ as the truth and the light that will never change. When the troubles of this world weigh heavy upon our hearts, Chapman exhorts us to turn our eyes to the Savior, remembering what He's done for us and holding on to what He's bringing about in us. Chapman also encourages us to allow ourselves to find our strength in Him through prayer and obedience and to ponder the value our souls have to Christ, having a thankful heart for His grace and forgiveness.

Tracy Chapman

Chapman seeks the righting of wrongs via truth and justice, attacking the materialistic "man-made white world" and its establishments for its racism and disregard of the poor and underprivileged. Condemning those who unjustly persecute or abuse others, Chapman invokes the specter of judgment, warning that "somebody's gonna have to answer." She sings of being devastated by those whom she trusted and cautions against being completely vulnerable because humanity is fallen and therefore perfection cannot be expected. Chapman notes her own sinfulness, as well, seeking forgiveness and reconciliation for her wrongs and searching for freedom and peace from the things that imbalance and upset her. Notably, as she demonstrates universal human imperfection, she reacts imperfectly, refusing to be hurt again and asserting that "I'll love myself more than anyone else." In regard to justice, instead of trusting God to reveal the truth with His light, Chapman seems to threaten and rationalize reactionary violence. As for her own soul, she acknowledges and denounces Satan but adds that she'll save herself.

Chumbawamba

The British octet Chumbawamba has just become recognized stateside even though they've produced several albums over some fifteen years. Notoriety was gained because of the group's "Tub-thumping" single. After listening to this cut one might assume that Chumbawamba is all about having fun and enjoying life. Not so. The vast majority of its lyrics are pointed political statements that promote anarchy and assert that all governments are repressive and tyrannical (a "tubthumper" is one who undermines authority by circulating subversive information). They envision a utopian existence full of "freedom" and devoid of accountability. Pro-drug themes are visible.

Paula Cole

Cole's musical focus has shifted to self-realization and self-assertion. She tells of escaping her constricting, narrow upbringing and embracing a new Paula Cole, one who is no longer fearful or timid and who celebrates life for what it is rather than what it could or should be. Cole expresses deep-seated pain, rage, and bitterness toward those who have been unsupportive, distant, or destructive. She furiously confronts Christ, asserting that His truth is irrelevant and turning her back on Him: "You walk the road to resurrection, and I walk the road to dead." One touching memorial is apparently written for an AIDS victim. Lyrics contain profanities and graphic sexual imagery.

Collective Soul

Collective Soul is wisely direct and discerning. Their lyrics glorify love as greater than anything else and display it as a choice rather than a feeling or an impulse. Collective Soul exhorts us to seek the truth relentlessly while allowing love to find us. Songs include odes to freedom, hope, patience, courage, equality, and acceptance. Others offer startlingly vulnerable glimpses into mental/emotional/spiritual pain, confusion, and loneliness. When wounded, Collective Soul extends forgiveness, while they reject reconciliation if it is to come at the expense of moral integrity. Lyrics also occasionally request that others allow for time, space, and understanding as a damaged heart learns to heal and to love. Collective Soul calls for us as individuals to be responsible and to assume accountability for our lives. While arguably at times the group's philosophy/theology is not entirely orthodox, they focus on the truth, and in so doing they give glory to God, for all truth belongs to Him.

Shawn Colvin

Colvin is sorrowful and weary for innocence lost and hope deferred. Lyrics share dreams of freedom and happiness tempered with a skeptical and discouraged message formed by Colvin's experiences. Frequent references to salvation point to inner emptiness and pain and perhaps suggest frustration with God for allowing her to be confused. Some songs contain profanity.

Coolio

Coolio's supposedly good intentions are overshadowed by his character flaws. He refers to abstinence as "abstersh——," telling kids to use condoms instead. He apologizes to women for names he's called them and ways he's treated them in the past, promises to treat them differently, and then on the same album uses vulgar references for parts of their anatomy and seeks to use them sexually. He steps out against marijuana on one hand but sings of being drunk and high on the other. He highlights the perils of gang life and then endorses the lifestyle. Coolio's music is profane and approving of violence.

Counting Crows

The Counting Crows recount tales of loneliness and fear, sharing a true sense of grief and loss and almost begging someone to prove that they care about them. Unhappiness and gloom is the prevalent theme as the band seems to determine there is no real escape from terror and depression. The Crows seem to experience heartrending pain that surfaces when attempts are made to demonstrate love. Some lyrics contain vulgar expressions.

The Cranberries

The Cranberries' content, while very different from one project to another, is consistently insightful and brilliant. Their first album,

"Everybody Else Is Doing It, So Why Can't We?" affirms devoted love, forgiveness, emotional vulnerability, and intellectual honesty. Lyrics are particularly poignant with regard to relational openness amid confusion, doubt, anger, disillusion, and anguish. The Cranberries' second effort, "No Need to Argue," highlights a fundamental struggle for identity that includes an unexplainable emptiness of the soul and a determination to hang on to a sense of hope for love, peace, and significance. Certain cuts denounce the unnecessary tragedy brought about by continuous warfare in Ireland, and demonstrate the wrenching pain and loss occurring from fractured relationships. The group's third release, "To the Faithful Departed," confronts dark and memorable elements. Lyrics, again, rise in anger and impatience against worldwide warfare and needless suffering, rallying to challenge mind control and trumpeting individual human freedoms. Some questionable utopian sentiments include confusion as to who and what should be glorified and admired. Yet such inquiry is clearly pro-communication and anti-violence.

Another song vehemently denounces drug abuse and suggests that use or non-use is the difference between slavery and salvation. While carrying inner turmoil over relational difficulties resulting in loneliness, and deeply troubled by the dishonesty and fickleness of others, lyrics still exalt forgiveness and patience, clinging tightly to a hope for the very best in every other human soul.

Crash Test Dummies

The Crash Test Dummies seem to extract and point out the absurd in everything and then find ways to laugh about it. However, while it's easy to write off or ignore such cynics and satirists, CTD's lyrics often shed a great deal of light upon the common mind of today's Generation-Xer. Lead vocalist (and primary songwriter) Brad Roberts is unquestionably well educated; the reason most of the lyrics appear shallow and surface-level in content is that when one becomes overwhelmed by the magnitude and frequency of the problems and difficulties of life, there are only so many options.

The Crash Test Dummies have chosen to poke fun at failure and mock the absurdity of life, thereby "conquering" it in the sense that pain is ignored and struggle is overlooked. One central belief of the band is that humanity has no special significance; that is, we're just like every other creature, and if anyone tries to convince you that we can have a personal relationship with God, you'll know he/she is missing a few bricks. Amid cryptic philosophical and spiritual allusions is the general idea that God is past His prime and is completely out of touch with today's world. The same goes for His Word, which bears no relevance for the things we grapple with from day to day. Some songs contain vile sexual allusions.

Sheryl Crow

Crow reflects upon desperate searches for love and significance, both angry and forthright and exceedingly dark and fearful, and yet somehow hopeful. *People* magazine (September 12, 1994) reported that Crow had terminated an engagement, and that her Christian fiancé had hoped that she would devote her musical career to the Lord. Her lyrics portray a dazed and disoriented soul wondering if anything is real, if anything can be called truth, and if any relationship can ever endure. Crow screams for peace, justice, and freedom. Crow's serious battles with depression and despondency have given her a persona of openness, and her insights often relate to her own experiences. Some songs contain profanity and references to substance abuse.

The Cure

The Cure combines mesmerizing numbness and apathy with bouts of heartache and loneliness. Deep emotional struggles are stunted by the myth that it's bad for men to be expressive and vulnerable. This results in depression as well as distorted views of self and others. The Cure sings about Christian faith at times but clearly doesn't hold that there is anything that's necessarily worth believing in.

[Comment: A band like The Cure, as depressing as they seem, actually makes some valid points about human nature and its tendencies. However, the answer is not to continue to look inwardly and live a life that revolves around self. This only makes things worse because we can't fix ourselves, and we become discouraged and doubtful when focusing on problems that seem hopeless. By contrast, we need to turn our eyes toward Jesus Christ, the one who alone can change our lives.] Lyrics include violence, sexual allusions, alcoholism, profanities, and implicit endorsements of death and suicide.

Cypress Hill

For Cypress Hill, frustration and anxiety spawn and validate violence, murder, obscenity, lewdness, and drug abuse.

dc Talk

dc Talk is about absolute, uncompromising devotion to Jesus, proclaiming and rejoicing in His faithfulness in spite of our failures. They repeatedly remind us that He is our only source of hope and that we are utterly lost apart from Him. dc Talk also asserts that since we are all forgiven sinners, saved by grace, we ought to love like the One who showed us what love is. This love is to cross all barriers and boundaries—we are not to look down upon or judge anyone. dc Talk confronts our selfishness, pride, and myopia in anguish, pleading for the unconditional extension of the love of Christ and the opening of our eyes, ears, minds, and hearts to the world's need for a Savior.

Depeche Mode

Depeche Mode (French for "fast fashion") has maintained steady popularity by focusing on the themes of sex and spirituality. Lyrics portray a soul constantly seeking identity through sexual activity and desire. Having tried nearly everything, he admits in "It Doesn't Matter Two" that sex is not ultimately fulfilling but he cannot find a better solution. Religious imagery is everywhere amid sad, nihilistic cries that God isn't here and only death is waiting.

"Cares" insists, "I have to believe that sin can make a better man." "Personal Jesus" suggests that Christ is whoever one needs him to be. Heartrending confusion and bitterness are revealed on "Blasphemous Rumors": "Girl of eighteen, whole life ahead of her, fell in love with everything, found new life in Jesus Christ; hit by a car, ended up on a life-support machine. Summer's day, as she passed away, birds were singing in the summer sky. Then came the rain, and once again, a tear fell from her mother's eye. I don't want to start any blasphemous rumors, but I think God's got a sick sense of humor, and when I die I expect to find him laughing."

Lyrics contain references to immoral sexual involvement.

Celine Dion

Dion in many ways captures the essence of love like few other artists. At times using both emotional and spiritual imagery, she presents love as intimacy, loyalty, sacrifice, passion, forgiveness, and endurance. Dion laudably points out that life without love is nothing; she renounces pride and selfishness and esteems love in action above promises or possessions. Dion lyrically places her faith in love, fate, and self. However, while at times experiencing loneliness, heartache, sadness, and confusion, she contrasts love and fear, rejecting self-pity and relying upon hope, courage, and resilience. Dion takes a mixed stance on abuse, frequently insisting that it won't be tolerated; daring men to learn to love, but at times suggesting that some things are worth enduring in the hopes that better circumstances will someday evolve. Dion does infrequently affirm that casual sex is acceptable. Some lyrics contain sexual references.

Dr. Dre

Dr. Dre endorses living for money and living without discipline or compassion. His music is boastful, obscene, hateful, and violent.

Missy "Misdemeanor" Elliott

Elliott employs frequent obscenity and blunt innuendo to invite noncommittal sexual involvement. She seems to base relationships on money and sex. Much of her material is tribute to her own success and superiority. Lyrics endorse marijuana use.

Enigma

Enigma (Michael Cretu) uses unique rhythms, beats, and chants to present intermingled theories involving transcendentalism,

Christianity, dualism, shamanism, and Eastern meditation. Cretu, an atheist, has said that he writes "moods" rather than "music," adding that his focus is not "sexual but sensual . . . there's a big difference." Vivid portrayals picture internal struggles with emotions and ideals: guilt versus freedom, love versus hate, love versus lust, and choice versus feelings. In a Virgin Records press release Cretu posits, "Old rules and habits have to be rejected so that something new can be created." He also suggests in *Rolling Stone* that "the institution of the church doesn't really fit with our times. I believe in destiny, which is a much more powerful belief." In "Sadeness" Cretu ponders the sexual philosophies of the Marquis de Sade, for whom sadism is named. In "The Principles of Lust" Cretu advocates Aleiser Crowley's doctrine of doing whatever one desires.

En Vogue

En Vogue (Cindy Herron Braggs, Maxine Jones, and Terry Ellis, now minus Dawn Robinson) endorses self-respect, honesty, responsibility, peace, unity, and color-blindness. The group has professed faith in God and has addressed Jesus Christ as Lord and Savior. Telling tales of and denouncing deception and betrayal, En Vogue encourages relationships based upon loyalty, patience, sacrifice, passion, faith, sincerity, and forgiveness. En Vogue rejects bitterness, fear, and hatred, embracing hope, love, and healing. One caution: On occasion En Vogue overemphasizes sex appeal. Some lyrics contain sexual innuendo related to unmarried sexual activity; one song contains profanity.

Enya

Enya's earlier works place great emphasis upon Celtic heritage, legend, and folklore, while liner notes mention various religious and mythological themes, from the bringing of Christianity to Ireland by St. Patrick to tales of ancient and medieval Gaelic and Druidic custom. Later lyrics contain possible astrological and spiritist references, and more than once Enya appears to question the effectiveness and validity of searching for meaning in these ways. While she is often tagged as a "New Age" artist, Enya is an Irish Catholic.

EPMD

EPMD's bravado and gang-related territorial posturing has less profanity than much music of its genre but is notably devoid of positive, relevant messages. Lyrics contain lurid allusions and endorsement of marijuana use.

Erasure

Erasure expresses dismay due to widespread discord, violence, and alienation in relationships. In response, it calls for peace, unity, and understanding. Erasure has also sought approval through its affirmation of gay sexual preference. Lyrics use spiritual imagery to describe and give tribute to love, passion, and emotional sensation in a continuous search for significance. Erasure looks around and sees chaos and confusion, which leads to questions as to whether God is real and true and whether there is hope for the world. Pain stemming from disagreement, separation, and abandonment is revealed as the source for the building of protective barriers around the heart in efforts to avoid further hurt amid struggles with bitterness and resentment. Lyrics contain sexual innuendo and astrological inferences.

Melissa Etheridge

Etheridge sings of love from a homosexual viewpoint, communicating such issues as sadness, faithfulness, angst, desire, loss, rejection, ecstasy, bitterness, dedication, hope, and isolation. She frequently speaks of temptation or desire as of or related to the devil. *The Advocate* (July 1994) quoted her as saying, "In the hierarchy of reincarnation, the lowest form is a heterosexual man. Then as you go up the ladder, the highest form is a lesbian." Lyrics contain sexual expressions.

Everclear

Overcome with despair and sadness, Everclear has tried in many ways to escape depression: alcohol, sex, money, and drugs. Songs recount the pain of hearing others mock those who are mentally ill, the loss of identity that comes from trying to live to please someone (or everyone) else, and the shattered heart of a child who's been abandoned by her father. Everclear coarsely communicates its hollowness, unable to find significance and love. Two conclusions are that a merciful God cannot exist if a child's mother can have a nervous breakdown and that AIDS is not God's damnation of anyone. Everclear is raw pain set to music.

Faith No More

Faith No More is a frustrated band that is based upon bitterness and confusion. In their lyrical worldview, life is ironic and absurd as well as lonely. Puzzling spiritual imagery enters their music, and at times it is difficult to understand Faith No More's view of God from its lyrics. More visible, according to David S. Hart, is the band's choice to name its publishing company Vomit God Music. Hart also explains that one of Faith No More's vocalists featured a favorite T-shirt on the cover of *Spin* magazine that depicts Jesus Christ masturbating in the Garden of Gethsemane. Lyrics contain profanity and sexual allusions.

4 Non Blondes

4 Non Blondes is sadness, confusion, and a desperate search for significance and meaning. Lyrics virtually cry out, "Who are we? Is this all there is? Isn't there something else—something better? Please help us!" The pain and the chaos are shown to be so pervasive that any escape seems welcome. Some lyrics include profanity.

Foxy Brown

Foxy Brown seeks to gain notoriety by displaying boasts and taunts regarding her prowess. Her lyrics include profanity and blunt, lewd sexual references.

Kirk Franklin (Nu Nation)

Franklin presents a worshipful celebration of Jesus as Sacrifice and Savior, admonishing us to hope in Him and depend completely upon Him, for nothing can overcome Him. Franklin praises God for

His mercy, creation, love, grace, joy, peace, and forgiveness. Lyrics
also offer prayers for blessing and for the presence of the Spirit.

The Fugees

The Fugees combine anti-establishment political rhetoric with
variable religious observations and inferences. While they are no-
ticeably well educated and acquainted with spiritual teaching and
doctrine, they seem to adhere to a strange and untenable combination of Rastafarianism and Christianity. The Fugees favor the use
of marijuana but speak out against other drugs. Their lyrics frequently contain coarse references, obscenities, and violence.

Warren G.

Warren G.'s lyrics have little content other than gangsta rhetoric,
obscenity, lewdness, and abuse.

Garbage

Garbage (Shirley Manson) embraces misery and depression.
Wounded and betrayed, the soul portrayed in Garbage's music feels
trapped in a hated cycle of pain, rage, and fear. Much speculation
regarding God and Satan, good and evil seems to decide that the
struggle between the two ends with evil victorious as the greater
power. Self-loathing results, along with a sense of being damned to
depravity.

Lyrics contain violence and sexual innuendo.

Geto Boys

The Geto Boys criticize interracial malice among blacks and condemn a cultural system they view as corrupt and blind. While they
utter some intriguing political statements, their content is ethically
inconsistent and irresponsible. The Geto Boys' obscene and vulgar
lyrics contain taunts and threats of violence and murder as well as
repeated references to unacceptable attitudes toward, and treatment
of, women.

The Gin Blossoms

The Gin Blossoms share depression and sadness, searching for love through sex, and seeking a reason to live amid all the confusion and loneliness. Alcoholism is the escape of choice; former member Doug Hopkins committed suicide after being removed from the band for his excessive alcoholism. Subsequent lyrics seem to suggest that life is worth living as long as one knows he is needed and loved. Some songs contain profanity and sexual imagery; one mentions palm reading and tarot cards.

Ginuwine

Ginuwine exploits sexuality. Some lyrics praise commitment and honesty and make it clear that pain and sadness come out of being betrayed and abandoned. Most of the lyrical innuendo isn't delivered in the context of a marital relationship. Songs contain substance abuse, profanity, and graphic sexual references.

The Goo Goo Dolls

The Goo Goo Dolls portray fearful and hopeless individuals overwhelmed with inner devastation and emptiness and feeling irrelevant, lonely, tired, and small. Mostly they perceive themselves as mentally and emotionally dead; when feelings do come, they're usually in the forms of sadness and rage. They sing of escaping through alcohol but reject suicide as an acceptable alternative. Lyrics contain profanity and sexual imagery.

Amy Grant

Grant has developed unique and refreshing ways of sharing the love of Christ. Most recently she has broached areas uncommon among Christian artists, including nostalgic sadness and relational miscommunication and separation. Grant praises marriage and family, endorsing sacrificial love and devoted friendship. While at times puzzled and discouraged by human nature, she encourages hope and perseverance through darkness and confusion and asserts that we must choose what is right and true no matter what our circumstances. Grant also points out that beneath our layers of self-protection we're all searching for love and security. She presents the positives of experiencing, rather than stuffing, our emotions, suggesting that they can lead us to healing. She declares that questioning and seeking God will be accompanied by revelations of His love and mercy. Finally, Grant urges us to step into action and make a difference when we observe needs and voids in the lives of others.

Green Day

Green Day dedicates its attentions to unacceptable attitudes toward public behavior, disrespect for and disregard of elders, alcohol and drug abuse, and indiscriminate sexual activity. Evidence indicates that the primary motivators, sadly, are self-hatred and loathing, general boredom, and disillusion with life. In response, Green Day has chosen to take rebellion to its extremes, adopting immaturity, profanity, and apathy as its foundations.

Hanson

Hanson's lyrical content is inspirational. The trio encourages faithfulness and honesty while exhorting listeners to be committed to and appreciative of those who are truly nearest and dearest to the heart. [Comment: Those who enjoy Hanson will want to remember that material regarding romantic love between men and women isn't something that needs to be a primary focus as we mature from childhood to adulthood. Also, don't forget that our worth is not derived from our real or perceived attractiveness to the opposite sex.]

Polly Jean (P.J.) Harvey

Harvey's extraordinarily expressive thoughts often focus on one woman's struggle to accept her femininity and embrace her personal identity. Harvey frequently seeks relationships in different forms; these end in various ways. Sadly, she is often wounded rather than built up through these involvements. She uses vivid metaphors for sexual concepts and at times uses somewhat unsettling spiritual terms and phrases. Some lyrics contain profanity, graphic sexual expressions, and alcohol abuse.

Dru Hill

Hill's music is devoted almost exclusively to romantic love. Much of his lyrical content is affirmation of such timeless virtues as faithfulness, gentleness, thankfulness, honesty, and mutual surrender. Likewise, the majority of Hill's music is best suited to those who are (or are committed to be) emotionally and relationally mature. Otherwise, the intensity of such romance can become distorted.

Hole

Hole's Courtney Love, widow of former Nirvana vocalist Kurt Cobain, sings of feeling hollow, lost, cheap, and disregarded. Raging and desperate, she rails against a world she believes is full of phony images and façades, communicating hopelessness along with confused, distorted pictures of her identity. Love is a paradox of personality: While at times appearing to be as hardened as diamond, she often communicates with vulnerability and pain. In addition to her husband, she also lost Hole's bassist, Kristen Pfaff, in a drug-related death. Lyrics contain profanity and graphic sexual allusions.

Hootie and the Blowfish

Darius Rucker and his cohorts highlight perpetual pain and sadness without succumbing to rage, apathy, or despair by encouraging hope and faith. Many frustrations and disappointments are expressed along with resulting numbness or grief. The key element for Hootie and the Blowfish is that it's not wrong to be willing to face and admit the difficulties of life; in fact, we need to. Second, though just as important, we must find a way to remain soft and caring in the midst of such hardships. The band lyrically values companionship, fidelity, and prayer, especially in the form of asking questions of God. Some lyrics refer to alcohol abuse.

Ice Cube

Ice Cube laments the woes and misfortunes of those forced to live amid poverty and crime and seems to have been shocked or numbed into a tragic apathy by what he has seen. Ice Cube claims to be "color-blind," but unfortunately his music is filled with racist sentiments. In addition, he includes boasts of murder and intimidation as well as sexual abuse of women. Lyrics contain profanity and lewd expressions.

Ice-T

Ice-T's lyrics confront a socio-political system that he believes ignores the poor and blankets the truth about the way they live by silencing them when they try to speak out. His exposé uncovers the illusion that we live in peace, demonstrating that unimaginable horrors are occurring constantly just outside our sheltered fortresses and bubbles. Ice-T has many premises that on their own are worthy of attention; unfortunately, he infects his music with violence and immoral activity in order to assure that more people will listen to it. He refuses to act in union with a culture he sees as being deceived and lulled into apathy, but in reply, he shirks responsibility for his actions and those he endorses by claiming that society has forced people like him into violence, drugs, and crime. He advocates a revolution based upon hatred and rage. Ice-T's lyrics are profane and graphically vile.

The Indigo Girls

The Indigo Girls assert that they trust in "a lesson learned, a loving God, and things in their own time." When emotionally vulnerable, lyrics detail sadness, anger, loneliness, shame, heartache, and confusion. These are countered by encouragement to hold on to love, strength, hope, nostalgia, and freedom. The Indigo Girls present an uncommon amount of biblical expression and spiritual speculation, reflecting a search for truth and also both a desire for and a disappointment with Jesus. Their music expresses life and love from a homosexual point of view, and while they condemn racism and ethnic insensitivity in all of its forms, they accept fear and hatred of gays without retaliating in kind. Lyrics contain references to, but do not frequently focus upon, pantheism (God is in everything), profanity, fortune-telling, astrology, reincarnation, sexual imagery, pornography, and alcohol abuse.

Iona

Iona blends original compositions with traditional hymns and Celtic liturgy to celebrate the unchanging faithfulness of God amid an errant and fallen world. Iona proclaims the primacy of wisdom as truth and light, encouraging listeners to seek the face of God and to request guidance, patience, love, protection, and faith. Against sorrow, discouragement, and fatigue, Iona lifts up the suffering of Christ on our behalf, the indwelling presence of the Holy Spirit for believers, and the hope of eternity.

Jamiroquai

For Jamiroquai, life is nothing short of insanity; existence is chaos. This politically astute group makes environmentalist and pacifist appeals while projecting a pantheistic approach to intelligence and action (the idea of the "force," for example). They also confront American civilization and government for its roles in settling and conquering this continent and for its allegedly selfish and tyrannical policies, calling for revolutionary change in perspective and practice. Jamiroquai produces music that is consistent with a continuing search for "eternity" or significance. To them, life is beyond comprehension—so much so that the only option for sanity is to close one's eyes and imagine and/or hallucinate. The only law (other than scientific law) recognized by Jamiroquai is desire, as expressed in "If I Like It, I Do It." Unfortunately, for them, "heaven" is sexual communication.

Janet Jackson

Janet's music is now primarily about sexual desire and expression. This, however, is not a celebration of the love God created to be enjoyed between husband and wife. It is an invitation to explore and fulfill sexual fantasy, regardless of relationship. Songs feature odes to situational, oral, and public sex, while videos depict her pawing and stroking her dancers, and a recent album cover featured her naked above the waist, her breasts covered only with a pair of male hands. This is a marked departure from some of the themes she emphasized earlier in her career and is just one indicator of the choices that the music industry presents to artists as an acceptable option to sell more albums and have a greater influence.

Michael Jackson

Jackson, arguably the most recognizable figure in popular music, speaks out against pride, abuse, racism, war, corruption, greed, and unscrupulous media. Conversely, he touts faith, love, peace, confidence, hope, and active responses to wrongs and needs as the necessary bridges toward his vision of human unity. Jackson's life has remained troubled by scandals and accusations. Often his sensitive heart seems saddened by the horrors around him and confused by the various struggles within, and his continuing searches for niche and identity either motivate or are motivated by (or both) constant scrutiny and criticism from others. Some lyrics contain profanity, sexual expressions, violence, and drug abuse.

Jars of Clay

Jars of Clay is a tribute to the joy, strength, and peace that come from knowing Jesus Christ, and the emptiness and heartache that result in a life apart from Him. Jars of Clay also sings of the need for forgiveness, vulnerability, and faithfulness between us as frail and fallible humans, lifting Jesus up as the One who brings us together and chooses to use us despite our fears and doubts.

Jewel

Jewel's sophisticated and passionately reflective themes sear into the heart's depths with wrenching remembrance and regret. Insightful and perceptive, they also celebrate honorable virtues such as honesty, faithfulness, and gentleness of soul. She makes pleas for unconditional acceptance and cries out for a presence of love, lamenting that people seek it in alcohol, sex, and drugs. At times she both angrily and vulnerably communicates pain and rage. Jewel mentions a man she used to sleep with, occasionally inserts profanity, and includes a bit of verbal crudeness in her liner notes.

Jodeci

Jodeci (half of which is the Hailey brother duo that comprises K-Ci & Jojo) has moved away from earlier roots in Gospel music and Boyz II Men-type appeal toward what they call "sexual R&B." Although they praise love that consists of devotion, sacrifice, and faithfulness and sing of the joys of passion and family, they round out the rest of their musical content with a slough of sexual innuendo, including endorsements of pornography, multiple-partner sex, and other tales of conquest. Jodeci has run into numerous problems in living out its sexual philosophies; while the band blames the media and an additional movement by "groupies" to ensnare and accuse young black artists to earn financial settlements from them, Jodeci has pleaded guilty to criminal sexual conduct. Lyrics contain obscenities and graphic sexual imagery.

Elton John

Many do not realize that Elton John generally puts other people's words to music (for example, most of the lyrics are written by his long-time cohort, Bernie Taupin, including the original "Candle in the Wind"). The words of his songs often capture love and beauty with strong emotional thoughtfulness. Amid realistic affirmations of life as pain and suffering, these words plead for hope, simplicity, peace, and harmony. They share a struggle with weariness, resentment, and confusion. Some lyrics contain profanity.

Unfortunately, it is hard for many people to separate Elton John's lyrics from his bisexual and former drug-filled lifestyle (see chapter 3 on lifestyles). They view his worldwide acceptance as an artist as somehow heroic. So while some songs may portray commendable themes, discernment must be used before granting wholehearted acceptance.

Montell Jordan

Jordan's "Daddy's Home" is a time-halting, beautiful apology for being a dead-beat father. Most of the rest of Jordan's material pays homage to irresponsible sexual activity, any time, any place—anyone? Lyrics contain profanity.

R Kelly

Kelly's music is an unfortunate paradox. Lyrics approve of both commitment and adultery; they also smile upon both monogamous relationships and irresponsible sexual activity. Kelly invokes both the "Good Book" and the Qu'ran. He sings of seeking God and paradise but regards a woman as heaven and says, "What does it profit a man to gain the world and lose his soul? I'm gonna trade it to be with you." Kelly also challenges people in the ghetto to change in order to make a difference, but then he subsequently endorses behavior that won't change anything. Lyrics contain profanity and graphic sexual language.

KORN

KORN displays two sides of the same tragic coin: the first is rage, frustration, and hatred; the second is pain, torment, and fear. Struggles with drug addictions have been wrought from anguish over being mocked and teased for being different and from fury over being abused and deceived while vulnerable. KORN portrays inner confusion and blindness; one heartrending song tells of a child being raped by his father. Lyrics are obscene and perverse.

Lenny Kravitz

The sometimes puzzling theology and worldview of Lenny Kravitz is revealed in various spiritual references that aren't always easy to interpret. What is clear is that while Kravitz is angry and pessimistic about the conditions of life (including war, prejudice, crime, drugs, and the government), he believes in the providence of God and the saving work of Christ. He repeatedly points to the end of time and begs his listeners to place their faith in Jesus. Kravitz resents those who claim to know and seek God and then bring war and death to humanity and to the earth. However, he is one of very few artists who appeals for peace without threatening violence or retaliation in kind. Kravitz exalts love, promoting dedication, vulnerability, healing, forgiveness, and sacrifice while acknowledging his personal shortcomings and showing a desire to change. Kravitz presents a dire warning against heroin use; his view on marijuana is less clear. Some lyrics contain profanity and sexual expressions.

Kris Kross

Kris Kross has come of age, but very little of what they have to say promotes maturity. Lyrics contain references to illicit sexual activity, belief in self at the expense of truth and wisdom, abuse of alcohol, kids carrying weapons, and rough language.

K's Choice

K's Choice is primarily a struggle with emotional questions— is it better to feel what's inside or to shut down and become numb? Is anything made to last? Are broken relationships (or the possibility of them) worth the pain they bring? Pointedly honest lyrics display an inner longing for love and acceptance. "Dad" is a beautifully poignant reflection of a child's lifelong love for her father and her desire to understand and be close to him. "Not an Addict" is about experience with drugs; it claims that "it's not a habit, it's cool." Some songs contain lewd or graphic allusions.

Jonny Lang

Blues child *wunderkind* Jonny Lang portrays both a healthy distrust of human nature and a high view of the possibilities of love. Relational themes focus upon desire, separation, perseverance, and dishonesty. "Good Morning, Little School Girl" is a kind of raging hormone anthem.

Annie Lennox

Lennox vulnerably expresses nostalgic thoughts and emotions amid relational frustrations and conflicts, including sadness, depression, euphoria, fatigue, disappointment, peace, loneliness, and the fear of rejection and abandonment. Lyrics proclaim the joy of motherhood, demonstrate regret over past mistakes, and exalt love over money, sex, and drugs. Lennox seems to reject salvation through Christ, although she shows an awareness of personal sinfulness and speculates on immortality and the future. Some songs contain sexual expressions.

Live

Live's fundamental question is, "Where did life go wrong?" Everything seems crazy and confused, and everyone is numb and lonely—there must be more to life! We *must* be worth *something*! Live sees our culture as lost, hollow, and overcome with sadness. They place some of the blame on the previous generation, blasting the notion of free love and decrying our isolation from and rejection of one another. Live also acknowledges some responsibility, determining that peace and rest are fleeting but that God is not the answer because meekness is the opposite of strength. Live thus opts to reject the "drama of heaven and hell" and vows to earn salvation rather than accept it from an allegedly powerless Savior. Live expresses terror at what they believe must lurk inside of themselves, deciding to adopt the conviction that we are all born confused and will die the same way. Live displays distorted sexual identities and fantasies.

LL Cool J

LL Cool J's efforts are less abrasive than those of many of his contemporaries, but they are still permeated with profanity, violence, and sexual activity without consequences.

Lost Boyz

The Lost Boyz confront the difficulties of ghetto life, lamenting its tragedies, observing its pointlessness, and calling for fundamental change. They also occasionally praise such qualities as faithfulness and intimacy. Lyrics, though, glorify illicit sexual activity and implicitly reject non-marital abstinence in exhorting listeners to use condoms as they endorse multi-partner sex. The Lost Boyz encourage marijuana use, boast of murder, and speak with obscenities.

Madonna

Madonna's well-known forays into and expressions of virtually every sexual possibility have brought her both various levels of fame and notoriety and sharp, enduring criticism. But she doesn't think she's more obsessed with sex than anyone else. She sees hypocrisy in a society that supposedly represses its "perverted" sexual fantasies and acts as though they don't exist.

Q magazine (December 1994) states, "She is for openness, believing it the opposite of ignorance; and if ignorance begets bigotry and guilt, so openness will bring happier times for all." Madonna says most of her critics are after her because "powerful women are a threat in any society." She has said that women are not allowed to "empower themselves without being labeled heretical and perverse." Along these lines, she claims to have had several abortions.

Basically, Madonna seeks to uncover the sexuality in everything. She views Catholicism in general as "kinky" and told *Spin* magazine (June 1985) that "crucifixes are sexy, because there's a naked man on them." Overall, in a 1995 interview with *New Music Express*, she says, "I think we all have the same God. . . . God is in all of us and we all are capable of being gods and goddesses. That's my brand of Catholic mysticism. Throw in some Buddhism and you've got my religion." Madonna also sees herself as a survivor. She says that losing her mother at a young age was the most powerful influence on her life; she reveals, too, that she was raped when she was young.

New Music Express (December 2, 1995), in speaking for her critics, says that what she calls "artistic expression," they call "masturbating on stage"; while she calls *Sex* "a book to promote debate about sexuality," they call it "porn." It's hard to misunderstand some of her own clear statements. She has said, "Straight men need to be emasculated. . . . Every straight guy should have a man's tongue in his mouth at least once" (*New Music*, May 27, 1991).

In regard to a picture in her *Sex* book, she responds, "Where the two schoolboys are attacking me, and I'm wearing my Catholic schoolgirl's uniform? . . . It was just another fantasy of mine, being overpowered. . . . There are a lot of women who have that fantasy where they are overpowered by two men or a group of men. . . . Everybody wants to do it. I have a smile on my face because I'm having a good time."

Ultimately, Madonna views herself as a cultural model who will one day be vindicated. She asserts, "My comfort is that all the great artists since the beginning of time have always been completely misunderstood and never fully appreciated until they were dead. They didn't understand Van Gogh, and they crucified Jesus Christ" (*New Music Express*, December 1995). Lyrics contain profanity and graphic, distorted sexual imagery.

Makaveli
(See 2Pac—Tupac Shakur.)

Marilyn Manson
Marilyn Manson, "Antichrist Superstar," appears as evil personified, producing the music of death: "I eat innocent meat; the housewife I will beat; the pro-life I will kill; what you won't do I will." Manson claims to represent Satan and seems to stand for everything that is objectionable.

Behind the façade is a tormented and anguished man who thinks his life is a mistake and that he is destined to be nothing but obscene, perverse, and blasphemous. Marilyn says, "I am the face of piss and sh—— and sugar. . . . I hate what I have become to escape what I hated being" and "I scar myself you see; I wish I wasn't me; I am the little stick; You stir me into sh——; I hate therefore I am; G—d— your righteous hand." While his devotion to hatred and malice will bring some to denounce Marilyn Manson as nothing but a sinister voice of darkness and despair, even this empty and raging soul needs to see the unconditional love of the Savior he despises. (Band members each take a famous female celebrity's name as their first and a famous serial killer's name as their last.)

Master P
Master P fills lyrical space with unimaginable tales of drug sales and abuse. One hobby is to sexually abuse women who are willing to be exploited as long as their addictions are taken care of. Master P reveals much despair over the state of the ghettos but suggests that change will not come because people have given up hope. The difficulty of living without fathers is referenced, as is frustration

over crimes committed against fellow ghetto residents (that is, they shouldn't be murdering members of their own ethnic heritage). Master P's expletive-filled material boasts of rape and murder and threatens gang violence and retaliation.

Matchbox 20

Matchbox 20 exhibits a fearful soul who feels small and overwhelmed and can't escape from inner shame that feeds (or is fed by) a poor self-image. Much attention is given to relational frustration that demonstrates ongoing battles between love, hatred, and apathy. Some lyrics contain profanity.

Dave Matthews Band

Certain songs are highlighted with calls to remember and assist the disadvantaged and underprivileged and to be true to ourselves by honestly expressing our emotions and thoughts. The Band gives a general acknowledgment of the difficulty of life, and lyrics frequently reveal a wish to find ways to lighten the dreariness of the mundane. It is to be noted that the outlet of choice for the release of the Band's pent-up frustration and energy is often illicit sexual activity.

Maxwell

Maxwell sings about passion, romantic love, and difficult struggles with emotions and relationships. Lyrics contain graphic sexual expressions.

Loreena McKennitt

McKennitt weaves a historical and mystical quest in search of the mysteries and meanings of the human need for spiritual fulfillment. She uses literary, monastic, mythological, scientific, and other ritual sources to journey through the various cultures of the Celts, Jews, Christians, Moslems, Chinese, and Japanese. Though not a "rock" musician (she is classified by some retail outlets as "folk" music), she is very popular with fans of artists such as Enya.

Sarah McLachlan

McLachlan's works reveal a startling intimacy with and comprehension of the ongoing state of the soul, including debilitating pain resulting from difficulties in relationship and profound woundedness out of being deceived. There is clearly a longing for true communion marked by openness and vulnerability with another soul. McLachlan leaves unanswered the question of her relationship to the man of whom she sings. Some might also feel she does not adequately resolve the painful issues she broaches. At any rate, it is probable that only those of mature heart and developed mind are capable of discerning and evaluating the contents and meanings of McLachlan's lyrics. Some contain profanity.

MC Lyte

MC Lyte's music is composed largely of boasting about her popularity, superiority, and eternality (apparently self-perpetuated). Lyrics include frequent profanity and coarse sexual references. One intriguing song chronicles the "game" of fleeting fame played by popular entertainers.

Megadeth

Megadeth portrays angry and bitter souls trying to make sense of confusion and chaos and to interpret a future that appears hopeless and fearsome. Megadeth laments social woes and evils and denounces war, crying out for peace but acknowledging that it won't come. Why? Because they know and understand enough of what has been prophesied regarding the end, which they have in their sights. Amid myriad scriptural expressions mixed with mythological references and mentions of satanism, divination, and sorcery, Megadeth desperately gropes for explanations, implicitly dreading death and judgment but mocking Christ as a failure and rejecting His offer of salvation. Lyrics contain profanity, violence, and sexual imagery.

Natalie Merchant

Merchant, of 10,000 Maniacs renown, sings of the benefits of perseverance, faith, and patience. She laments the tragic death of

River Phoenix, mourning that he couldn't be saved from himself (he died of a drug overdose). Lyrics also reveal that she questions whether she has closed herself to truth, and she seeks to escape inner confusion and uncertainty. She beautifully depicts a man's unbreakable love for his wife and painfully recalls being left by her own love, at times displaying brokenness and at others bitterness.

Metallica

Metallica is, at the same time, anger and hate, intelligence and insight, hopelessness and despair, wisdom and wit, folly and fear. While frequently raving of death and of rage, spirituality is the main focus of this group. Lyrics reveal a terror of the knowledge of the depths of the human soul, while chaos and insanity accompany unmistakable affiliation with thoughts and emotions. Spiritual anguish and torment are clearly visible as Metallica repeatedly gives reason for listeners to hold on to the idea that they do not believe they are in control of their own souls. Other insidious entities (demons are often cited) allegedly hold the keys, increasing inner torment and confusion with a horrifying and unhindered inertia. Pain is regarded as relentless and never-ending; lyrics appear to question whether there will ever be hope for release and renewal.

Metallica points out the emptiness of selfishness and warns listeners not to mess with things that are evil, suggesting that they have no idea what they might be getting themselves into. Lyrics withhold the fieriest of hatred for those who judge and condemn others and the sharpest of ridicule for the alleged mindlessness and dependency of many believers. Jesus is seen as a broken promise because of His death; in heartbreaking verse, Metallica deems Him "the god that failed." Lyrics contain obscenities, threats of violence, and references to suicide, which on occasion is endorsed.

Mia X

Mia X wields taunts of violence and murder while otherwise concentrating on profanity, graphic sexual allusion, and various genres of abuse.

George Michael

Michael has moved from a direct, graphic focus on sex to deeply rooted emotional issues and spiritual questions and longings. While he still suggests that he prefers casual sex over promised commitment, he claims to have been changed to a degree by his experiences. Now he seems to carry enough pain from the consequences of past involvements to say that true love isn't worth the risk of betrayal or abandonment. Michael rejects the finding of identity and fulfillment through fame, and he curses greed and pride for the corruption they bring. He encourages kindness and support between friends, and he continues to seek answers for his difficult, probing questions regarding God and life.

Michael grieves bitterly over war and the world's cruelty, singing "So, if it's God who took her son, he cannot be the one living in her mind." "Praying for Time" represents Michael's tragic conclusion that amid our fallenness God has lost control of the world and that somehow, to our utter dismay, hope has been lost. Some lyrics contain profanity and sexual expressions.

Ministry

Ministry spews murderous hatred and vengeance toward those who have done them wrong, furiously confronting a confusing world and all the nonsense and irrelevance that accompanies it. Ministry reserves special rage for comfortable, conservative America—its obsession with possessions and its mindlessness in dealing with the media. Lyrics imply an overwhelmingly negative view of self, probably best illustrated by the song "Filth Pig." Ministry frequently editorializes upon morality and damnation, and while graphically perverse and blasphemous, denouncing God and distorting His truth, Ministry is searching for a source of light.

Alanis Morissette

Morissette's voice is one tormented and vexed, crying out for peace, fulfillment, and a love that is true and unconditional. Acute woundedness from being used and rejected screams out in anguish and raging bitterness, furiously demanding justice for the wrongs

done to her. She sings of brokenness and shame from the weight of
the demands and expectations of her parents, and she lambasts the
Catholic Church she sees as insincere and artificial. Morissette is at
times vividly perverse and profane.

Aaron Neville

Neville exalts friendship and romantic love, endorsing support,
sacrifice, and faithfulness in both. His lyrics comprise nostalgic cel-
ebrations of love and life. They express grief and sadness for relationships broken and grateful indebtedness to those who love and
have loved generously and without condition.

New Edition

New Edition (including Bell Biv DeVoe) sings about relationships, groovin', and sex. Relational sentiments include pleas to hold
on to love and requests for forgiveness. One song thanks God for
His protection and provision. Some lyrics contain profanity and
graphic sexual imagery.

The Newsboys

The Newsboys boldly proclaim Jesus Christ and point to Him
as the only way to salvation and the only source of hope. They assert
that we are to place our faith in God and then obey Him—if we
choose to believe in Him, the only reasonable option is to be fully
sold out for Him. The Newsboys denounce shame and condemnation as defeated foes, highlighting God's grace and mercy. Lyrics ex-
hort us to be the Lord's light in a lost, dark world; they also present
the indwelling Spirit as our means for holiness and love. Likewise,
we are to reject bitterness and apathy, forgiving as Christ did and
praying for renewal from fatigue and frustration and for strength
against temptation and despair.

Nine Inch Nails

Trent Reznor of Nine Inch Nails lyrically shares his anguish,
rage, depression, and confusion, revealing that he feels hopelessly
lost, depraved, and hardened but still experiences enough emotion-

ally to be driven nearly insane. He expresses his unbearable fear of being controlled: "I speak religion's message clear (and I control you); I am denial, guilt, and fear (and I control you); I am the prayers of the naïve (and I control you); I am the lie that you believe (and I control you). I take you where you want to go, I give you all you need to know; I drag you down, I use you up; Mr. Self-Destruct." Words of sarcasm and cynicism only accentuate his hatred and terror as he desperately gropes for a sense of identity through sex and music. Spiritually, Reznor seems to have moved from shock and bewilderment to full-fledged fury in his quest for truth. "Terrible Lie," written early in his career, reflects his confusion as he confronts his Maker: "Hey God, I really don't know what you mean. Seems like salvation comes only in our dreams. I feel my hatred grows all the more extreme. Hey God, can this world really be as sad as it seems? . . . You made me throw it all away. My morals left to decay. How many you betray. You've taken everything. . . . My head is filled with disease. My skin is begging you, please. I'm on my hands and knees; I want so much to believe. . . . I give you everything, my sweet everything. Hey God, I really don't know who I am in this world of piss." "Heresy," written later on, mirrors his heartbreaking contempt and more visible hatred: "He sewed his eyes shut because he is afraid to see; he tries to tell me what I put inside of me. He's got the answers to ease my curiosity; he dreamed a god up and called it Christianity. . . . He flexed his muscles to keep his flock of sheep in line; he made a virus that would kill off all the swine. His perfect kingdom of killing, suffering, and pain demands devotion—atrocities done in his name. Your god is dead and no one cares; if there is a hell, I'll see you there." Lyrics contain profanities, graphic violence, vivid sexual expressions, and possible endorsement of suicide.

Nirvana

Nirvana (formerly led by deceased singer Kurt Cobain) portrays life as one of terror, anguish, and boredom. Lyrics scream a cry for help and direction. They attack a culture they see as self-righteous and judgmental and yet unhelpful, wallowing in bitterness and hatred at being used and misunderstood. Nirvana's graphic imagery reveals deep sadness and loneliness along with a sense of feeling forced to glue the pieces of life together and act as though everything is okay. In an existence of nothingness, worthlessness, and mindlessness, drugs are said to provide the only reality, and suicide the greatest hope. Nirvana wonders who should be blamed for their mental/sexual/emotional confusion—God? Culture? Parents? Themselves? They suggest that life is out to destroy them: "Just because you're paranoid don't mean they're not after you."

No Doubt

No Doubt (Gwen Stefani) exhibits surprising lyrical depth; some songs even comprise a general parody of living shallowly and without purpose. No Doubt celebrates the uniqueness of individuality and the importance of harmony, affirming that while we are all beautiful and different, we must know that we were made to work together and to learn from one another. At the same time, No Doubt also displays evidence of a soul so wounded as to question whether mutual trust and respect between individuals is possible in actuality. Honest and vulnerable expressions of pain and loneliness demonstrate frustration with feeling deceived, used, unimportant, and without value. There is a generally observable change in No Doubt's music over time that reflects maturing and deepening values and emotions.

The Notorious B.I.G.

Biggie Smalls' unfortunate musical heritage is obscenity-ridden art endorsing murder, gang violence, group sex, and drug abuse. It's also saturated with references to indiscriminate sexual activity and raunchy, lurid suggestions.

Oasis

The music of Oasis is a tribute to the perceived lack of man's need for God. The band believes that man is improving and that the world is getting better. Consequently, man will continue to reach new heights and will live forever (on earth, so the idea goes). Oasis gives two main guidelines for life. The first is selfishness. What oth-

ers need is irrelevant; take care of yourself. Find happiness and fulfillment (alcohol and drug abuse is the recommended solvent). The
second is apathy. Don't care about anything you can't control (which
is everything but yourself), because opening your heart to love will
only steal your soul. While the façades of Oasis are arrogance and
pride, the substance is the same as for any whose hearts have not
been touched by Christ: fear of lostness and terror of hopelessness.

The Offspring

The Offspring is a well-educated albeit angry band that seeks to
open our eyes and minds to the absurdity, cruelty, and circularity of
life. Filled with rage and indignation with America's political and
cultural structures for their alleged myopia and execution of injustice, The Offspring endeavors to undo our societal "blindness." In
an *RIP* interview (October 1994), Offspring member Dexter Holland
says, "Parents are easy to piss off, so that's always fun to do. . . . That
whole culture, the religious right, is just so full of sh———."

At times, The Offspring vulnerably provides glimpses of emotional and spiritual turmoil, sharing struggles with loneliness and
emptiness, forgiveness and bitterness, low self-esteem and confusion, and the pain of fractured relationships. The problem, though,
is that the solution The Offspring offers for our "mindlessness" is
only further blindness. Endorsing selfishness and denying absolute
truth, The Offspring appeals for cycles of hatred and apathy, singing
that "the more cynical you become, the better off you'll be." Lyrics
contain obscenities, threatened violence, graphic sexual imagery,
and endorsement of marijuana use.

Joan Osborne

Osborne's combination of spiritual and sexual inferences is frequently cryptic and difficult to interpret. Her lyrics indicate that
confusion and doubt are being coupled with both a questioning
search for truth and an unchanging standard by which to live. "One
of Us" seems to cry out for a God who is personally oriented and
accessible, reflecting weariness and disillusion with caricatures of an
austere, disconnected, and disinterested Deity. Osborne also high-

lights the despair of depression and hopelessness, admitting that she feels depraved and lost and frequently turning to such desperate measures as immoral sexual activity and drug abuse in her quest to find significance.

Ozzy Osbourne

Osbourne, once of Black Sabbath, presents a musical world inundated with religious and spiritual imagery, displaying opposing forces of good and evil in a continuous war of cosmic proportions. While God is frequently invoked, probed, and questioned, Satan is repeatedly drawn as an insidious and more controlling power. Here the battle becomes personal, as Osbourne explains the devil's incessant torture of his soul and cries out for respite from the torment of demons and voices. He details his struggles with shame, defilement, weariness, hatred, desperation, blindness, lust, and insanity as he laments violence, evil, and death.

Osbourne's material frequently projects his spiritual insights. He tells of the eternality of the human spirit, singing that "there are no unsavable souls" and "there is religion to cover my sins." However, he also claims that "there are no believable gods," "there are no undisputed truths," "there are no forgivable sins," and "I'm not a son of Christ." Osbourne propels scathing critiques of judgmentalism, self-righteousness, and religious hypocrisy. While he was once an abuser of alcohol and drugs, Osbourne reportedly broke free on the day he says he heard God tell him to "Quit today, or you will die." Lyrics contain profanity, pro-suicide messages, sexual innuendo, and occultic references.

Pantera

Pantera (Spanish for "panther") displays mortally wounded and bitter souls, raging and hateful of themselves along with everything and everyone else. Particular fury is aimed at God; lyrics filled with scriptural imagery blaspheme the Lord and denounce His Gospel. *Metal Maniacs* (August 1992) cited lead vocalist Phillip Anselmo as saying, "Something I find unbelievably stupid is putting the fear of God into kids' heads. Making him [the kid] watch his every footstep his whole life, to cater to an afterlife. . . ." Pantera advocates escape from life through alcoholism and drug abuse (Anselmo experienced clinical death before being revived after a near-fatal experiment with heroin). Lyrics contain obscenities, violence, endorsement of suicide, and vile, graphic sexual language.

Pearl Jam

Pearl Jam is a representative voice for innumerable souls wondering if there is anything truly worth living for. Dark, reflective, and broken by struggle and confusion, lyrics sometimes portray an individual merely waiting for whatever end is to come, mourning the loss of innocence and desperately longing to be able to satisfactorily feel and communicate. Often angry, occasionally frustrated, and always lonely, Pearl Jam at times seems to reject intimacy and trust because it is suggested that the desirability of these will imminently become outweighed by the high costs of pain and betrayal.

At other times, it is evident that lyrics suggest that the only thing one can truly put one's trust in is music. While the band's theology is often confusing and frequently inaccurate, Pearl Jam displays a genuine struggle to understand the power of the flesh over the soul in experience, hardly daring to hope that there might be a chance for redemption. Indeed, shame and sadness are evident as lyrics demonstrate an eye-opening awareness of personal fallenness and unworthiness. Pearl Jam, while often not drawing godly conclusions from its inquiries, is music that is frantically grasping for something—anything—that will prove itself faithful and true. Lyrics contain profanity and coarse references.

Liz Phair

Phair represents herself with fury and power. If one looks a bit more closely, what is visible is a soul who was been immeasurably damaged, particularly by sexual involvements. If her words in "F—— and Run" are to be taken at face value, she started being active in and being hurt by sex when she was not yet a teenager. Her response to feeling manipulated and used is quite human: She now takes matters into her own hands, having adopted a raging, retaliatory approach to sexual activity. Hopefully, only love and compassion will be shown to Phair by followers of Christ. It's important to acknowledge, though, that we can't make wrongs right by acting wrongly ourselves, which Phair embraces in her music. Abuse and control is wrong no matter who is responsible for it. Lyrics contain profanities, alcohol and drug abuse, and graphic, perverse sexual language.

The Pharcyde

The Pharcyde's cleverly penned wordings and unique sense of humor are not compatible with their lyrical profanity, drug abuse, violence, and lurid accounts of sexual activity.

Point of Grace

Point of Grace displays the immeasurable work of Christ's sacrifice and reveals him as Lord and Savior—the focal point of existence. Nothing is impossible with Jesus, and there is grace enough for everyone to embrace His love for us. Point of Grace calls for love, forgiveness, and evangelism to initiate the unity envisioned and made possible by Jesus Christ, who made known to us the person of God and redeemed us so that we might come to believe on Him and live in Him. Point of Grace also urges Christians to maintain their Christlike example, motivated by the grace and mercy God gives, along with the hope of a new eternal home.

Porno for Pyros

Perry Farrell (formerly of Jane's Addiction and of Lollapalooza renown) has made a tragic career of experimenting with religion, sex, and drugs and sharing his adventures with others. Sadly, his musings on relationships and life in general are warped and chaotic; his emotional and spiritual speculations are absurd and distorted. This is possibly due to his extensive drug abuse and dealings with the occult. He ignores and/or rejects anything of truth and value and purposefully searches for ways to deviate from what is right and honorable. "Porno for Pyros" is drawn from Farrell's tale of being stimulated to masturbation by the thrill of the L.A. riots. Lyrics contain obscenities, violence, graphic sexual imagery, and drug abuse.

Portishead

Portishead seems to repeatedly ask one underlying question: Is there anything to believe in and live for? Portishead presents a soul with a timbre of loneliness and fatigue, beset by fear, discouragement, and confusion. Their promising view of love is for them tainted by painful experiences, and their very dim portrait of life is augmented by the idea that life *is* pain and only death itself will bring relief. Portishead appears to be very alert to both personal and general human sinfulness.

The Artist, formerly known as Prince

The Artist's music speaks for itself, sadly bringing to the forefront and endorsing the perverse depths to which the human soul can allow itself to plummet in its search for life.

The Prodigy

Prodigy is in Great Britain what Marilyn Manson is in the U.S.— ultimate shock and unprecedented energy. Prodigy is profanity, anarchy, and terror; certain band members are so frightening in appearance so as reportedly to cause children who see them on TV to burst into tears of fear. Keith Flint, the lead singer who is covered with what look to be satanic tattoos, was quoted in a *Daily Star* interview as saying that by the time he retires, "I'd like to say I bedded tons of babes and lived out my ultimate sex fantasies."

Puff Daddy

Puff Daddy (Sean Combs) overcame the pain of losing his friend Biggie Smalls to eventually record another album. Combs recalls the pain of witnessing that murder, along with others when he was younger, and questions both what life is worth and where it's going. His music endorses murder and violence and is filled with profane gang-related taunting and threatening. His material is degrading of women in general and consistently includes lurid sexual imagery and action. He rationalizes this lifestyle by citing ghetto conditions, and he claims that his inspiration to continue producing in the industry is the life of the Notorious B.I.G., with whom he agreed that they "rhyme with God," in other words, speak on God's behalf.

Queen Latifah

Queen Latifah calls for the respect long overdue to African-American women, questions the meaning of life and its cruelty, and also delivers general taunts regarding her superiority. Latifah encourages listeners to use condoms during casual sex, which she endorses. She suggests at other times that people should be friends and love each other before they have sex. Lyrics contain profanity and sexual language.

The Queers

The Queers are so named because they "just wanted something that would piss people off." They claim that there's "no deep message" in their music—it's about "being f——ups" and "having fun." But that's not entirely true. While at times they do step into a zany state and write songs like "I Can't Stop Farting" and "I Only Drink Bud," most of the time, whether they believe it or not, they are quite serious.

The Queers use sarcasm, parody, and an "everything is irrelevant" façade in an attempt to deal with and cover over inner hatred, self-loathing, anger, and fear. Sadly, the Queers have a very low view of humanity in general and of themselves in particular. The Queers actually do become temporarily vulnerable when singing of love and security, but then they seem to snap into a different frame, one that mocks and perverts everything it touches. This serves to distance the band from appearing to have feelings and desires. Lyrics contain obscenities, violence, graphic sexual and anatomical imagery, and endorsements of alcohol and drug abuse.

Radiohead

Radiohead exhibits life as fearsome, chaotic, and absurd, once mocking God for all the pain that exists, and deriding those in positions of authority, suggesting that standards and rules only cause more disorder. Lyrics showcase low self-esteem and almost beg for affirmation and acceptance, agonizing over isolation and indifference, but deciding that sincerity and emotional effort merely serve to intensify the pain of life. Some lyrics contain profanity.

Rage Against the Machine

Rage Against the Machine comes out against the culture in fury, demanding justice for wrongs they believe have long been established and perpetuated by the dogmatic "Right": the government, the media, the church, and the other forces of capitalism. According to the band, these agencies, throughout the history of the development of the United States of America, have controlled and brainwashed us by distorting the truth and making illegitimate appeals to the presence of fear and the loss of safety. Consequently, individual freedoms have been eradicated, the populace has become ignorant, and other cultures have been virtually destroyed. Livid because of unnecessary wars and other unjustifiable games allegedly played by the tenacious élite of the political and social status quo, Rage Against the Machine calls for a violent revolution against the illicit "American dreams." These are said or implied to be: Eurocentrism, compromise, submission, Manifest Destiny, élitism, ignorance, conformity, hypocrisy, brutality, and assimilation. Lyrics contain profanity.

Rancid

Rancid's music tells a tragic history of being abused, impoverished, and abandoned. It is also the tale of trying to find a way to overcome the resultant pain through substance abuse and immoral activity. No solid answers appear, and the products of life are loneliness and sadness. One song is an ode to suicide; many selections are profane. Rancid does believe that humans are in control enough to make decisions regarding their destiny. As for itself, Rancid says, "Relatives of mine said they were born again; F——ed-up world has made me born against; I'm a sinner and my soul should be cleansed; I'll take my chances when I'm dead."

The Red Hot Chili Peppers

The music of the Red Hot Chili Peppers portrays personal slavery to drives and desires and reflects self-loathing with terror of further self-discovery. Empty and depressed, bitter and angry, their lyrics rage against God: "I was not created in the likeness of a fraud. Your hell is something scary; I prefer a loving god. . . . Shallow be thy game. Two thousand years—look in the mirror. You play the game of shame and tell your people, 'Live in fear.' . . . You'll never burn me, You'll never burn me. I'll be your heretic; you can't contain me. I am the power free; truth belongs to everybody. To anyone who's listenin', you're not born into sin. The guilt they try and give you, puke it in the nearest bin." The Red Hot Chili Peppers call for the end of war and racial discrimination and the beginning of peace. Lyrics contain obscenities and lewd sexual imagery.

Reel Big Fish

Reel Big Fish uses a unique sense of humor to emit sarcastic, surface-level sentiments relating to music, popularity, interpersonal communication, fads, sexuality, and vegetarianism. For the most part, Reel Big Fish isn't really singing about anything of note, as a song such as "Beer" might indicate. "Everything Sucks" is in the genre of bored disillusion. Lyrics contain profanity and coarse sexual allusions.

R.E.M.

R.E.M.'s once impassioned messages of political and social awareness have been pushed aside for more personal expressions of disillusionment and depression. Outside of fervent, exploratory sexual energy, R.E.M. best describes the general tenor of its recent efforts in "Bittersweet Me." Singing of innocence lost and of a life that now seems dark, cold, and without promise, Michael Stipe laments, "I'm tired and naked. I don't know what I'm hungry for. I don't know what I want anymore." R.E.M. seems trapped between obsession with a life of fame and disgust for its emptiness. Some lyrics contain obscenities and graphic sexual imagery.

LeAnn Rimes

Rimes has recorded many inspirational renditions that highlight faithfulness, beauty, nostalgia, eternal hope, patriotism, and dedication. Songs that focus upon mature relational themes exalt love and romance while lamenting deception, lack of communication, and selfishness. Some have raised the question of whether or not a young teenager like Rimes should be singing about mature romantic themes and in the process implying that others of the same age group can or should experience such relationships.

Salt-n-Pepa

Salt-n-Pepa (Cheryl James, Sandi Denton, and DJ Dee Dee "Spinderella" Roper) bring confidence, self-respect, and sexual expression to the forefront with their pointed cautions about lifestyle and their vivid references to sex appeal. The group has made pleas for making a distinction between what they portray in song and what they live in action. In an interview with Lorraine Ali, Cheryl James says, "Gangsta rap and crazy sex in rap music became popular because we *made* it popular, the same way we can make something else popular. . . . Let's not act like gangstas on record, then act like that in real life, too. Let's say, 'That's me on record, and this is me in person.'" [Comment: That's irresponsible—listeners are impacted by the material whether the artists wish to admit it or not.]

Salt-n-Pepa encourage women to acknowledge and affirm their true beauty and value and to act accordingly; they also endorse "empowerment" of female sexuality, desiring that sex be viewed as "an equal-opportunity sport." Denton urges, "Get what you want out of the situation, and don't just be giving at your expense." [Comment: While there is much in their message that is to be endorsed, the godly response to being wronged is not to respond in kind. Sex is not a weapon to be given and withheld as punishment or reward; nor is it something men or women should control over and against the other. Retaliatory measures only perpetuate a circle of sins.] Other lyrics truthfully warn that sexually transmitted diseases aren't "black, white, or gay" phenomena; part of the advice given is, "Protect yourself or don't have sex anymore." Some songs contain coarse language and graphic sexual innuendo.

Adam Sandler

Sandler combines genuine hilarity and enjoyable satire with some of the most disgusting and vile lyrical content and commentary imaginable. Too bad—he wouldn't need to use profanity and perversity to be funny.

Savage Garden

Savage Garden is mostly about relationships: love, passion, romance on one hand, frustrations and struggles with emotions, role-playing, and betrayal on the other. Some lyrics confront deep-seated loneliness and pain and speculate as to how one might escape. Savage Garden seems to promote honesty and faithfulness. Certain sections contain mature imagery.

Scarface

Scarface (Brad Jordan) rages against the American law enforcement system for allegedly assuming the worst about people like himself and treating them like animals. Anguished, he highlights the pain and loss caused by violence and death in the ghetto, painting a grim picture of despair as he suggests there is no option but to steal and sell drugs to survive. Scarface can't understand why rappers are so heavily criticized for their musical content, declaring that nothing they produce is any worse than, for example, what's in western movies on TV. His lyrics are filled with obscenities and graphic sexual expressions and contain allusions to substance abuse and the degradation of women.

Seal

Seal (Sealhenry Samuel) is a unique and well-educated artist who frequently shares his views on the nature of the problems and virtues of humanity. His music is literally filled with spiritualistic references of various kinds. Much of it is inspiring and uplifting, touching on the glories of unconditional love and the wonders of compassion, sacrifice, loyalty, and peace. Seal even exalts the death of Christ: "It changed my life."

If there is issue to be taken with Seal's material, other than the varied sources of his spiritual investment (such as palm-reading), it is that he seems to place far more faith in man than in God. [Comment: Along these lines, a primary focus of Seal's optimism is, in truth, humanism. In modern times, humanism has come to embrace a distorted picture of the value of man without God—specifically, Jesus Christ. Hope is a wonderful thing, but it is no greater than the object in which it is placed. We must be zealous to be certain that the hope we possess is placed upon the only One who is worthy of it.]

Jon Secada

Secada focuses primarily on romantic love, often using spiritual imagery to glorify faithfulness, tenderness, forgiveness, and vulnerability. Secada laments relationships that have been lost, and he decries deception and betrayal. Some lyrics contain sexual expressions.

Silverchair

Silverchair chronicles the effects upon the soul of despondency, hopelessness, and shame. Lyrics tend toward one of two fundamental conclusions: one is hatred and bitterness, and the other is death, usually in connection with suicide. This young band demonstrates an acute awareness of the confusion and isolation of the lost soul; unfortunately, they choose to respond by focusing upon themselves rather than searching for a greater source of love and power. Silverchair painfully regrets what they perceive to be unnecessary death in the world around them and takes note of the sadness and despair of children who are abused or neglected.

Sister Hazel

Sister Hazel presents a man who struggles to fathom the depths of human emotion, nature, and desire. This man promises faithfulness while at the same time acknowledging the difficulties he has with commitments. Sister Hazel suggests that we ought to embrace the present while learning from the past in order to construct the future. Lyrics often showcase a soul looking for love and stability amid the loneliness and the sometimes overwhelming pace of life.

Smashing Pumpkins

Smashing Pumpkins' music is a grievous telling of the nihilism and emptiness through which much of today's world sees life. Existence is depicted as meaningless, the future as bleak and undesirable: "I lie just to be real, and I'd die just to feel. . . . Beyond my hopes there are no feelings. . . . Beyond my hopes there are no reasons." They express this because even though the band's lyrics contain some tributes to sincerity and lasting love, they also insist upon the pointlessness of love as unattainable and fleeting.

According to their music, the Smashing Pumpkins are looking for peace within themselves. They say this is found through significance in someone else's eyes; that is, to find another person who can connect with the awful loneliness: "I can't help but feel attached to the feelings I can't even match. . . . It's wonderful to know that you're just like I." Sadly, though, they seem to have decided life is void, and everything true and good is but a dream: "Emptiness is loneliness, and loneliness is cleanliness, and cleanliness is godliness, and god is empty just like me—intoxicated with the madness, I'm in love with my sadness." Jonathan Melvoin of the Pumpkins died of a heroin overdose.

Smash Mouth

Smash Mouth promotes irresponsibility and endorses immoral sexual behavior under the guise of tolerance. The band is spiritually astute and emotionally alert, yet disregards all questions and obligations with a simple "F—— it, let's rock." Songs that provide realistic views into difficult issues could be insightful; instead, Smash Mouth runs roughshod over truth, denying the value of life and ascribing the same level of worth to animals and humans. Lyrics contain apparent endorsements of drug abuse.

Michael W. Smith

Smith laments society's moral and spiritual deterioration, pointing to Christ as the Savior and Lord who heals and strengthens. Smith believes every soul is seeking love and significance; he encourages obedience and prayer as a means of coming to know God and of grasping hope that extends beyond this lifetime. Lyrics warn against experimenting with sin and charge listeners to be faithfully devoted to one another to foster growth, holiness, and courage.

The Sneaker Pimps

The Sneaker Pimps portray a soul who has a dim view of life and self. One that feels confused, disillusioned, and hardened, who doesn't feel valuable; feels used and cheap. Generally melancholic themes use vague spiritual imagery to express a sad hopelessness and boredom with life. Some lyrics contain sexual innuendo and astrological references.

Snoop Doggy Dogg

Snoop's disillusioned lyrics comprise a survivalist approach to life; he suggests that he does what he does and says what he says to stay alive. His music is filled with lurid allusions to sexual activity and abuse, gangsta threats and taunts, and profanity.

Social Distortion

Social Distortion, like many artists, takes note of what they see inside of and around them and put it to song. They're different, however, from most others in that they consistently take responsibility for personal wrongs. They openly point out how profoundly we are impacted and shaped by our experiences, and they portray the real and sure consequences that will follow one's action.

Social Distortion sees themselves as both a cultural abnormality and that same culture's future. Low self-esteem is prevalent in frequent pictures of shame and disgrace. Social Distortion refers to both "God's holy grace" and of finding themselves, although they don't directly indicate whether for them these two are combined. Clues might be given in the form of regular references to prayer, the contrasting of faith and fear, and the biblical admission of "I try hard now to do the right thing, yet I wonder why I still do what is wrong." Perhaps they also indicate how they see themselves with their album title, "Somewhere Between Heaven and Hell."

Social Distortion often vividly displays pain and trauma, sobered and saddened by repeated close-up glimpses of this world's grief and suffering. They blast the "ignorant" and blind political, technological, and social structure that they believe oppresses the people with lies and twisted propaganda. They encourage supportive friendship while sending somewhat mixed messages regarding drugs. Lyrics contain profanity, violence, sexual imagery, alcohol abuse, and possible endorsements of suicide.

Soul Asylum

Soul Asylum (David Pirner) is about trying to help oneself and others to find their home and their identity. Soul Asylum's nobly honest and vulnerable insights often paint a bleak and sometimes hopeless portrait of a life filled with depression, frustration, misery, loneliness, desperation, and confusion. While the singer tells of feeling guilty and ashamed, he also feels misunderstood and disregarded. The earnestness of Soul Asylum's searching is enough to both break and empower one's heart: "Who can teach me how to change my ways; who will come and save the day?"; "How on earth did I get so jaded? Life's mystery seems so faded."; "We are not of this world, and there's a place for us. Oh, I'm so Homesick. I'm Homesick for the Home I've never had." Lyrics contain abuse of alcohol and drugs, rough imagery, profanity, and sexual innuendo.

Soundgarden

Soundgarden's music of depression and confusion vacillates from loneliness and sad isolation to anger and bitter recrimination. Lyrics indicate some form of obsession with darkness and death, and a general sense of personal insignificance permeates Soundgarden's content. Accordingly, the answer given is to focus upon oneself, adhering only to those standards that fit the individual. "Jesus Christ Pose" is a noteworthy song that comprises a partial portrayal of an unbeliever's image of Jesus. Lyrics contain a few rough references; one song contains profanity.

The Spice Girls

The Spice Girls' music is mostly about sex and making one's own rules. Primarily self-oriented, most songs are about getting, not giving. The Girls seem to take pleasure in frustrating men sexually and in participating in whatever sexual activity brings them the most pleasure whenever they want it. One song contains a touching tribute to motherhood.

Squirrel Nut Zippers

The Squirrel Nut Zippers speculate on various topics without making many assertions or drawing many conclusions. Areas of focus include love, individual identity, ethics, destiny, and hell.

Lisa Stansfield

Stansfield's musical focus is male/female love. Touching lyrics capture the passion and warmth of the marital relationship and the patience and sacrifice required to produce strength and intimacy. Sad portraits reveal the pain and separation wrought by unfaithfulness and abuse. Listeners will note that on occasion there is allusion to sexual activity outside of marriage and that overinflated expectations result in damaged hearts when a person's sole attentions are given to another person rather than to God. Lyrics include infrequent profanity.

Sting

Sting displays his vastly educated and knowledgeable mind throughout his lyrics, which reveal questions of the deepest kind, such as, "Who are we?" "What are we here for?" "Where will we go when it's over?" and "What should we be seeking now?" He touches upon the importance of dreams, encouraging the listener not to give up hope while both acknowledging and chronicling the devastation brought about by shattered aspirations. He seems to be angry when observing the discouragement and disillusionment in his fellow man and the difficult conditions with which they must contend, and wonders whether God is to blame. He sings vulnerably of his moral and ethical struggles, apparently clinging to one last source of faith, hope, and love, although it is not easy to tell what that source is.

Many of Sting's works contain political and social commentary. He recounts the horrors of war, decrying the tyranny and despotism of government, and trumpeting the cause and the future of the children we will leave behind.

Rebecca St. James

St. James exalts God as Father, Creator, and Savior, praising Him for His blessings and memorably challenging believers to fully surrender their lives to Him for His service and to His glory. She holds up love and prayer as preeminent, both in response to and in mirrored growth of a Christian's willful incorporation of God into every area of life. St. James exhorts her listeners to be separate from the world while not neglecting to share with it Christ's love and truth. She also encourages believers to love one another with the love of Christ—faithfully and sacrificially.

Stone Temple Pilots

The Stone Temple Pilots (Robert DeLeo and Scott Weiland) are disillusioned voices who struggle with whether life is hopeful or hopeless. They seem to wonder whether to forgive or to hate, to experience love and to feel or to become apathetic, to laugh or to cry—in short, to hold on or to let go. The band weathered severe criticism against their song "Sex Type Thing," which was allegedly a fantasy about rape. STP claimed that it was an ironic mockery of machismo written from the perspective of a date rapist. According to *Circus* magazine (December 30, 1993), Weiland's sexual philosophy is "Try to have as much sex as possible, because it makes for much more peaceful human beings."

There is a tragic and definite correlation between the band's difficulties with shame and with drug addiction. *Rolling Stone* (June 29, 1995) reported that after Weiland was arrested for drug possession, he released a statement that was read by Courtney Love over the radio, part of which said, "I have a disease . . . called drug addiction. . . . I'm sorry. . . ." Some of the Stone Temple Pilots' songs contain profanity, sexual imagery, and references to alcohol and drug abuse.

Sublime

Sublime's suggestion is that pain isn't worth confronting; it's much better to become emotionally numb by abusing alcohol and drugs. Sublime feels that humankind is ruining civilization with progress; that is, our technological advancements are erasing all the things that make the world a place worthy of our presence. These "things" aren't clearly defined, but Sublime does seem overwhelmed by the state of the culture. They speak out against marriage, declaring that it is an outdated institution and no longer workable in today's world. Lyrics contain profanity and vivid sexual allusions. Sublime's Brad Nowell died in 1997 of a heroin overdose.

Sugar Ray

Sugar Ray's angry material rejects truth, mocking Christ ("Jesus saves. No, he shoots, he scores.") and advocating immoral behavior as a response to a culture it sees as a farce. One song glorifies Mike Tyson and excuses his violent behavior. Lyrics contain profanity and graphic sexual references.

Suicidal Tendencies

Mike Muir of Suicidal Tendencies says, "I'd rather feel like sh—— than be full of sh——." He claims to be a scapegoat for society; that is, he says he is telling the truth about life, but that people denounce him because they fear the reality of that truth and can only deal with it by turning their backs on those such as himself. Raging and resentful, lonely and sad, Muir suggests that there are no answers in life; Suicidal Tendencies portrays absolute hopelessness and emptiness. [Comment: We are often quick to judge or to slander those who live this way. But the issue isn't convincing them that things really aren't so bad and that they should stop acting as though life is nothing but pain. The truth is that in and around some people evil has been so pervasive and overwhelming that they can't embrace anything else. The issue is praying for and compassionately helping these tragic souls, beloved of God, to realize that when their eyes are turned upon Jesus, their perspective will change and healing can begin.]

Keith Sweat

Sweat has gradually become more and more focused in his songs on sexual activity and energy. He tells of his devotion to love, and he promises to treat women well. However, for the most part, Sweat isn't singing about love but rather sexual prowess and conquest that degrades and devalues women for the fulfillment of his own desires. Lyrics contain explicit sexual material.

SWV (Sistas With Voices)

SWV sings about love, sex, and passion. Certain lyrics contain vivid sexual imagery and expression, some of which is explicit.

third day

third day is amazed at the mercy and grace of God. The band points to Him as the faithful giver and sustainer of life, and exhorts listeners to focus upon Jesus before anything else, encouraging prayer and praise. They proclaim the fiery indwelling of the Holy Spirit, endorsing a walk worthy of the believer's calling, and recognizing the joy that comes from knowing God's peace. Lyrics condemn gossip and hypocrisy while acknowledging personal sinfulness and turning to the forgiveness of the Lord. The band notes the health that flows from an individual's willingness to experience emotions, and bids the listener to hold on to hope in the midst of sadness, grief, and fear.

311

This group affirms the existence of a Creator ("Evolution is a f——ing stupid idea; we were created by God."), but seems to believe He is no longer active and involved with the world. They deny that there is any absolute truth other than their own desires; indeed, they advocate godlike status for themselves ("We're set to light your world, kid; we're your maker."). They also promote libertarian freedoms for all humankind (" 'Do what you wilt' shall be the whole of the law until you violate the rights of another."). Various references to theological or cosmic ideas such as reincarnation indicate a hodgepodge of different spiritual tenets. The group at times appears to adhere to somewhat conflicting philosophical ideals. On one hand, 311 attacks current musical trends toward negativism and encourages listeners to "stay positive and love your life." On the other, they say that "the more things stay the same, the more it doesn't matter."

They discourage the use of cocaine but promote marijuana. Ultimately, the paradox seems best resolved in concluding that while 311 believes in a god, this "god" seems to be (or to have become) the self or other people: "Be positive with life; see the god in everybody." Lyrics include frequent profanity and graphic allusions.

TLC

TLC embraces noble endeavors—and then immediately reinforces all the wrongs they supposedly set out to correct. TLC laments human fickleness—which, unfortunately, is exactly what they practice as they erotically tease their way from one desire (or man) to another ("Switch," for example). They condemn unfaithfulness and deception—and then ironically about-face and rationalize their own promiscuity ("Creep," for example). TLC decries the culture's sexual practices—and then offers only condoms as a cure. TLC's "sexual consciousness" is sexually irresponsible. Lyrics contain profanity and graphic sexual innuendo.

Toad the Wet Sprocket

Toad the Wet Sprocket paints an illustration of souls broken—lost and confused, angry and wounded, fearful and exhausted. The band openly shares their human side, singing, "It is hard to rely on my good intentions when my head's full of things that I can't mention." Toad the Wet Sprocket tells of unbreakable relational bonds and encourages faithfulness and forgiveness, yet they have become distrustful due to having seen so much of humanity's sinfulness and fallibility. Toad the Wet Sprocket grieves over the hurt that we cause one another and seeks ways to mend hearts and find peace. One song reveals the regret and shame of rape. The group's spiritual ideology is unclear, but they seem to suggest that we should embrace the acceptance of everything as mutually valid. [Comment: The main problem with this, of course, is that the only way to sidestep the fact that certain ideas and premises are in fundamental conflict with each other is to deny that a fixed, absolute standard of truth exists.] Some lyrics contain obscenities and violence.

TonyToniToné!

TonyToniToné! (Raphael Saadiq, D'Wayne Wiggins, and Timothy Christian Riley) express their desire for relationships based on personhood rather than on material desires. They also exhibit frustration and resentment over feeling used for their fame and money. They frequently sing about love and respect but sometimes speak very disrespectfully of women. Some lyrics contain sexual imagery, profanity, and violence.

Tool

Tool wears a grim mask of confusion and absurdity, but underneath are tormented souls who feel trapped in hatred and inner emptiness. Rage, terror, selfishness, and anarchy permeate bitter musings that repeatedly blast existence and mock Jesus. "Prison Sex" is about sodomy and retaliation; its recommendation is "Do unto others what has been done to you." "Opiate" accuses God of treachery and deception: "Jesus Christ, why don't you come save my life? Open my eyes and blind me with your light and your lies." Tool's music includes obscene and perverse sentiments.

Tru

Tru portrays the frustrations of ghetto life by demonstrating its hopelessness. Lyrics assert that there aren't any genuine opportunities, and that while corrupt politicians and police officers are overlooked, the poor and the underprivileged are hounded and pursued mercilessly, whether they've actually done anything illegal or not. Tru's response is that the only viable recourse is to live as a gangster—dealing drugs, administering violence, and generally getting hold of all that can be had before death comes. Tru's music contains profanity and graphic sexual references.

2Pac (Tupac Shakur)

Tupac's material is a consistent tribute to living without commitment and partying without constraint. He glorified alcohol and drugs as friends and immoral sex as heaven. Filled with vivid violence and lurid sexual expressions. A sad legacy. (Tupac has posthumously had music released under the name Makaveli, among others.) He died of gunshot wounds.

Twista

Twista expresses anger at being misunderstood and disregarded as worthless. Lyrics reflect a disillusion with a selfish and pointless world and a basic conclusion that God seems to have ordained life as Twista knows it. Twista displays gang violence, posturing, and murder while vividly narrating sexual activity, abuse, and brutality.

UB40

UB40, while often spinning "feel good" music that caters to fun and relaxation, also sees itself as a voice for the common people against corruption, greed, waste, and unnecessary gain. UB40 soundly criticizes self-righteousness, religious control, and bland utopian sentiment that lives in an insulated bubble and ignores the suffering all around, pretending that all is well and that peace reigns. While lyrics reveal a high view of love, romance, and passion as well as sacrifice and patience, forgiveness is given a bit of a bum rap as UB40 seems to delight in watching the tables turn on deceptive or insensitive former allies. UB40 sounds clear warnings against drugs. However, other lyrics contain sexual allusions, profanity, and alcohol abuse.

Usher

Usher (Raymond) uses the guise of "love" to front for images of profanity, violence, drug abuse, and various sexually explicit themes. Usher's choices seem somewhat incongruous with his stated beliefs (he addressed Jesus Christ as his Lord and Savior in his liner notes). "You Make Me Wanna" unintentionally illustrates part of the problem of lovers living together without being married. [Comment: People are mortally wounded when such a relationship ends because they have fully given themselves, body and soul, to someone they are not committed to for life and therefore have relinquished a part of themselves they will struggle to recover.] Lyrics contain profanity, drug abuse, violence, and sexually explicit language.

U2

U2 originally made its mark with vivid social commentary and piercing calls for humanitarianism coupled with an idealistic hope that real change was possible for the world. Their outlook was fairly bright, and they supported it with consistent appeals to the Christian faith and personal efforts to help and encourage those in need. Their last several albums, however, have indicated a distinct (although gradually evolving) change. While U2 is no less poignant, insightful, and maybe influential, they seem to have been hardened to a degree by several factors, thus becoming somewhat cynical and brooding. This seems in part to be explained by a sense of being overwhelmed and disillusioned with society's increasing influence on materialism and commercialism at the expense of substance— love, faith, truth, and hope.

U2 now appears to question both God and man. They suggest that we are to blame for our decadence, but in fear, frustration, and helplessness they also wonder whether God is no longer able to make a difference or is no longer interested in the world. U2 cries out to Jesus, who is seen, for whatever reason, as now separated from and possibly dead to His creation. Pleas to Jesus are raised for the aching needs of the soul for love and simplicity and for the consummation of a new era of history. U2 seems in some ways to be torn between living lives of temporal or eternal importance.

U2 has lyrically rejected sex without love as well as dishonesty, selfishness, and cruelty in relationships. Recent songs reflect Bono's regret for his original rejection of his mother and her faith, along with recollections of others' sad searches for and rejections of life. Some lyrics contain violence, profanity, and sexual imagery.

Van Halen

Van Halen, one of the most famous party bands in history, unfortunately fills most of its lyrical content with things that are harmful to the soul. The band sings a lot about love, but their type of "love" is abusive and degrades women. Van Halen also smiles on alcohol and drug abuse. More recently, they have displayed raging hatred toward Christ. Some lyrics are sexually explicit and contain profanity.

Jaci Velasquez

Velasquez combines a solid acknowledgment of life's difficulties with an accurate portrait of human nature. These come together to form a common assertion: our faith and focus shouldn't be upon ourselves but upon God. This God she paints as the Giver of healing, deliverance, shelter, providence, holiness, and strength. Velasquez presents a clear model of discipleship that includes prayer, humility, sacrifice, and purity. She also dreams vividly of her someday eternal home in heaven. She encourages the lost and lonely to turn to the God who brings love, hope, and safety, and she exhorts believers to realize that Christ has given us everything we need to share His love with a dying world.

Veruca Salt

Veruca Salt fills its music with emotions and reactions based upon rage, shock, anger, and passion. While the Chicago foursome's lyrics are often strangely vague and/or distorted, Veruca Salt is more about expression and noise than it is about significance and meaning. Some of the absurdity is possibly related to the band's involvement with such elements of the occult as seances, channeling, and

Ouija board. Lyrics contain violence, graphic sexual language, and obscenities.

The Verve

The Verve is a tired, empty, and lonely voice calling out for answers as to why life seems overwhelming and out of control. Trying desperately to cling to freedom and hope while grasping for love and joy, The Verve wonders if anything is absolute and unchanging; that is, worthy of our trust and faith. They seem to be undecided about drugs, claiming that they don't work but unable to offer a better solution (except music). One song vulnerably states, "Jesus never saved me; He'll never save you, too." One song contains obscenities; other lyrics contain sexual innuendo.

The Wallflowers

The insightful and often cryptic music of the Wallflowers reveals a fatigue of being wounded and lonely and a disillusion with the world's hatred and confusion. They convey a general aura of knowledge; the band's lyrics highlight educated minds. In connection with that knowledge, the Wallflowers display an awareness of and a sadness with the melancholy and pain of life and wonder, usually without drawing conclusions for the listener, what is to be done for today's lonesome soul. The Wallflowers seem not to be so much in pain or broken themselves as they are simply in touch with the climate of the society that surrounds them.

Weezer

Weezer (Rivers Cuomo) is lonely and desperate, searching for somewhere to belong but so overwhelmed that escape from his emotions seems to be the only acceptable possibility. In "The Good Life," he sings, "I should have no feeling, 'cause feeling is pain. As everything I need is denied me, everything I want is taken from me. But who do I got to blame? Nobody but me." Lyrics tell in sorrowful fashion of being devastated both by the pain he's caused others and the pain others have brought him. "Tired of Sex" speaks of the emptiness of his sexual adventures and of his desire for true love. Songs contain profanity, sexual imagery, and reference to marijuana use.

Westside Connection (& Ice Cube)

Westside Connection is profanity-laced rage and hatred, extolling gang-related power and violence. Lyrics are also filled with graphic and lurid sexual expressions.

White Zombie

White Zombie displays themselves as twisted and depraved, shock-rocking their way to renown and apparently becoming more vile with each dose of encouragement they receive from their supporters and each message of denunciation from stunned parents and religious leaders. Lyrics filled with satanic imagery blaspheme God and curse Christ, vilifying Him and portraying Him as demented and sick. White Zombie's music contains profanity, violence, and horrific sexual allusion.

Vanessa Williams

Williams has used the controversies that engulfed her after her Miss America and *Playboy* experiences to launch a popular career in music. Her odes to love glorify romance, commitment, passion, and forgiveness. Williams has chosen truth over blindness, honor over greed, and love over lies. However, she responds to betrayal by her significant other by quickly selecting and flaunting another lover of her own. Some lyrics include sexual imagery.

Wu-Tang Clan

While at times merely making raging and irrelevant noise, Wu-Tang Clan infects the remainder of its "music" with profane and blasphemous odes to its own prowess and virility, unacceptable attitudes toward and treatment of women, and graphic, perverse sexual imagery.

ZZ Top

ZZ Top has kept all of its original members together longer than any other rock band in history. At the same time, they haven't changed a great deal. Whether the music is about fast cars, good times, or wild women (adjectives are interchangeable), ZZ Top's work is inundated with sexual innuendo and allusion that is at different times fantasy, suggestion, and action. The pervasive element is the degradation of women by relegating their status to that of mere sexual objects.

Resources

Some Internet web sites for Christian artists

Music Central—http://www.netcentral.net/music.html

CCM Magazine—http://www.ccmcom.com

The 77's—http://www.77s.com

Altar Boys—http://www.wam.umd.edu/lbdavies/music/altarboys/abpage.html

Susan Ashton—http://susan-ashton.com

Audio Adrenaline—http://www.audioa.com

Margaret Becker—http://www.visi.com/keepon/mb.html

Bob Bennett—http://fly.hiwaay.net/jrinkel/bob

Ray Boltz—http://www.wordrecords.com/boltz/index.html

Caedmon's Call—http://caedmons-call.com

Michael Card—http://michaelcard.com

Carman—http://www.carman.org

Steven Curtis Chapman—http://scchapman.com/index.html

Christafari—http://www.christafari.com

Code Of Ethics—http://spring.eecs.umich.edu/jivey/code.html

Dakoda Motor Co.—http://place2b.org/cmp/dakoda

dc Talk—http://www.dctalk.com

Bryan Duncan—http://www.myrrh.com/duncan/index.html

Everybody Duck—http://www.public.asu.edu/robtarr/ebd/index.html

Glad—http://www.glad-pro.com

Amy Grant—http://www.myrrh.com/amygrant

Steve Green—http://www.gocin.com/stevegreen
Jars of Clay—http://www.jarsofclay.com
Phil Keaggy—http://www.museweb.com/keaggy
Wes King—http://personalwebs.myriad.net/banks/wesking
Crystal Lewis—http://rohan.sdsu.edu/home/galano/crystal.html
Mark Lowry—http://www.marklowry.com
Geoff Moore—http://www.geoffmoore.com
Cindy Morgan—http://www.wordrecords.com/morgan/index.html
The Newsboys—http://www.newsboys.com
Out of the Grey—http://www.ootg.com
Twila Paris—http://members.aol.com/Mazie20/twila.html
Janet Paschal—http://www.janetpaschal.com
Sandi Patty—http://www.wordrecords.com/patty/index.html
Petra—http://www.wordrecords.com/petra/index.html
Point of Grace—http://www.europa.com/llawson/point.htm
Resurrection Band—http://walli.uwasa.fi/mandt/rez/rez.html
Rebecca St. James—http://www.rsjames.com
John Schlitt—http://www.wordrecords.com/js/index.html
Michael W. Smith—http://www.michaelwsmith.com
Take 6—http://www.musictus.com/take6
Kathy Troccoli—http://www.nauticom.net/www/express/
    troccoli.htm
Jeni Varnadeau—http://www.pamplinmusic.com/jeni.varnadeau
Whiteheart—http://www2.southwind.net/scatcat/whpage.html
World Wide Message Tribe—http://www.message.org.uk

Index

About Steve Peters

Steve Peters is president of Solid Rock Ministries and author of the classic *Why Knock Rock?* He has appeared on ABC's *Nightline*, *Entertainment Tonight*, *The 700 Club*, and *The Sally Jessy Raphael Show* to talk about rock music. He has also spoken to over three million teens and adults in his multimedia presentations and authored seven books. He lives in Minnesota with his wife and two children.

A dynamic communicator for over twenty-five years, Steve Peters keeps youth and adult audiences riveted to their seats with his fast-paced, hard-hitting Truth About Rock seminars. Steve rips the mask off "harmless" rock music through his extreme visual multimedia presentation.

One of the best in the U.S., Steve Peters speaks to large groups at youth conventions, outreach rallies, city-wide and area-wide seminars, combined ministerial association outreaches, music festivals, school lyceums, and camps and retreats.

This eye-grabbing visual presentation confronts the lyrics, lifestyles, goals, and graphics of today's musicians while Steve compares and contrasts them with biblical passages that relate God's standards for our lives.

Over three million people have experienced his ministry, and thousands of participants vow to change their listening habits or commit their lives to Christ at the conclusion of his rallies.

Host his seminar and touch your city with this vital message. Many share that the Truth About Rock seminar was the largest, most productive event they ever sponsored. Teens and adults come by the hundreds, driving for miles and packing auditoriums to view this controversial production. All leave with a deep respect for Steve's well-documented research and an exposure to the presence of the Holy Spirit in their lives.

Thousands of moms and dads tell him, "You are the answer to our prayers for our desperate teen. Thank you for coming."

To receive a complete packet of materials on how you or your organization can sponsor a Truth About Rock seminar, please call or write. For $30, you will receive:

1. *A Complete Introductory Packet.* Complete details on what to expect, a list of references, bio, financial considerations, and procedures for scheduling an event with Steve Peters. Also included: sample poster, flyer, catalog, Truth About Rock Report Newsletter, and a personal letter introducing Solid Rock Ministries.
2. *"Rock Music, Good, Bad, or Ugly" Video.* Recorded at a live seminar, this video graphically reveals the truth about heavy metal, soul, thrash metal, and Top 40. 60 minutes. (Retail $29.95)
3. *"Why Knock Rock?"* A copy of this best-selling book on rock music that has sold 120,000 copies. 272 pages. (Retail value $9.95)
4. *"Sex, Violence, and Rock Music: Backstage with Rock's Meanest Bodyguard" Cassette.* "Big Chick" Huntsberry and the Peters Brothers go backstage to expose accounts of illegal drugs, sexual orgies, violence, death, and even murders at concerts. 60 minutes. (Retail value $9.95)

This packet is great to give to a pastor, school principal, promoter, youth worker, or potential sponsor who may be interested in hosting a Truth About Rock music seminar. These materials are perfect to share with small groups to promote Steve's upcoming rally, or to reach groups with this important message when costs prohibit a live seminar.

Call or write:

Solid Rock Ministries
P.O. Box 1004
Burnsville, MN 55337
(612) 892–6007
(612) 892–1012 fax

Steve Peters in the Media!

"Do you want an articulate spokesman and a program that people remember? Consider Steve Peters. . . . Everything good guests should be: concrete, full of good examples, unwavering in [his] conviction and flexible enough to work in any format. . . . If you have the opportunity to book him, do."

Mary Windishar, Producer
People Are Talking, KPIX-TV
San Francisco, CA

An articulate, thought-provoking guest, Steve Peters has done his homework and has gone toe-to-toe with hundreds of rock artists and DJs, holding them accountable for their lyrics and holding their feet to the fire of public scrutiny.

Invite him to be your guest!

He has debated Gene Simmons and Paul Stanley of the infamous rock band KISS. He's debated record executives on ABC's *Nightline* with Ted Koppel, appeared on CBS News with Dan Rather, tangled with rap's 2 Live Crew and drug-promoter Bud Green on *The Sally Jessy Raphael Show*, frequented *The 700 Club* with Pat Robertson, TBN with Paul Crouch, and many more.

He's been written up in *Rolling Stone*, *People*, *Time*, *Newsweek*, *Us*, *Charisma*, and *Contemporary Christian Music* magazines as well as *The Washington Post*, *The Minneapolis Star Tribune*, and many more.

Solid Rock Ministries (612) 892–6007
Bethany House Publishers (612) 829–2500.

Or write to:

Solid Rock Ministries
P.O. Box 1004
Burnsville, MN 55337

About Mark Littleton

Mark Littleton is president of Winsun Communications, pastor of Westbridge Church, and a frequent speaker at Christian gatherings. He is author of more than fifty books for children, teens, and adults, including a winner of *Campus Life* magazine's Book of the Year Award. Books authored by Mark include *Conversations with God the Father* (Starburst), *Get a Clue Mysteries* (Standard), *The NIRV Kids' Devotional* (Zondervan) and *God Is!* (Starburst). Littleton and his wife, Jeanette, live in West Des Moines with their three children and two cats.

Mark speaks on such subjects as "God: Your Greatest Friend," "How to Overcome Temptation," and "How to Grow Strong Through the Problems of Life." He can be reached for ministry considerations at (515) 226–0846.